Never Too Old to Get Rich

Never Too Old to Get Rich

The Entrepreneur's Guide to Starting a Business Mid-Life

KERRY HANNON

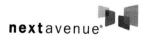

WILEY

Published by John Wiley & Sons, Inc., Hoboken, New Jersey.
Published simultaneously in Canada.

For general information on our other products and services or for technical support, please contact our Customer Care Department within the United States at (800) 762-2974, outside the United States at (317) 572-3993, or fax (317) 572-4002.

Wiley publishes in a variety of print and electronic formats and by print-on-demand. Some material included with standard print versions of this book may not be included in e-books or in print-on-demand. If this book refers to media such as a CD or DVD that is not included in the version you purchased, you may download this material at http://booksupport.wiley.com. For more information about Wiley products, visit www.wiley.com.

Library of Congress Cataloging-in-Publication Data
Names: Hannon, Kerry, author.
Title: Never too old to get rich : the entrepreneur's guide to starting a
  business mid-life / Kerry Hannon.
Description: Hoboken, New Jersey : John Wiley & Sons, Inc., [2019] | Includes
  index. |
Identifiers: LCCN 2019015620 (print) | LCCN 2019017755 (ebook) | ISBN
  9781119547945 (Adobe PDF) | ISBN 9781119547914 (ePub) | ISBN 9781119547907
  (hardcover)
Subjects: LCSH: New business enterprises. | Career changes.
Classification: LCC HD62.5 (ebook) | LCC HD62.5 .H367 2019 (print) | DDC
  658.1/1–dc23
LC record available at https://lccn.loc.gov/2019015620

V10010141_051019

For Jack

Contents

Contents

Foreword

Elizabeth Isele
Founder and CEO,
The Global Institute for
Experienced Entrepreneurship

No! "Senior Entrepreneurship" is not an oxymoron. The 21st century is the "Age of Experience" and that experience is driving social and economic change worldwide. Today's longevity is historically unique. There is no blueprint for what to do with an additional 20 to 30 years, but entrepreneuring seniors around the globe are designing their way into new lives, optimizing their life and work experience in nontraditional career paths and creating businesses of their own – from micro- to multimillion-dollar ventures – in unprecedented numbers.

For the past six years, I have been crisscrossing the globe, convening dynamic summits of world leaders in government, universities, and the private sector to raise awareness of the power of experience, and to convey the urgent need to build an ecosystem of innovative collaborations and new pathways, through technology and inclusion, to equip older individuals with the skills and resources they need to support and sustain an "Experienced Economy" (www.amp.com.au/amp/videos/releasingthepotentialoftheexperiencedeconomy).

At the summits, I share insights and best practices from country to country, such as:

- Finland is the first country to declare experience is its number one natural resource!
- A recent study in Spain revealed that for every €1 the government invests to mitigate the "retirement syndrome," it will receive a stunning €129 in return.
- In the U.S., the U.K., Ireland, and Australia, 50+-year-olds are launching more start-ups than any other cohort.
- The European Union has determined senior enterprise is key to achieving its 2020 economic strategic growth goals.
- In Japan, where I met with more than 500 business, government, and university leaders at the behest of the U.S. State Department, Prime Minister Abe has created a new initiative, "Agenomics," to harness the knowledge and resources of the largest and fastest-growing aging population in the world. More than a public policy, this initiative is being advanced through a number of university innovation centers, (public/private) business incubators, coworking spaces for start-ups, and finance agencies designed to support older entrepreneurs in this traditional business economy where the mandatory retirement age is still 60.

Today's older and bolder entrepreneurs, with their wealth of life and work experience, are particularly suited to succeed in our digital, big data, hyper-complex, Internet of Things world. Five key assets include:

- **Curiosity**: They thrive on ongoing learning and discovering new ways to make unlikely connections work.
- **Resilience**: They have failed in countless ways over a lifetime and have overcome many obstacles, so they have a high tolerance for risk.
- **Proactive, Positive, Practical Optimism**: They are eager to solve problems, and their life experience of knowing what works and what doesn't is a huge advantage over those who've spent little time testing new ideas.
- **Multidisciplinary**: Experienced individuals understand the benefit of reaching out to others from multiple disciplines, ages, and backgrounds for their insights. I recently heard this brilliant nugget, "Instead of multi-tasking, we should be Multi-Asking," in a short movie called *The Adaptable Mind.*

- **Empathy**: Be it selling an idea, product, or service, empathy is key. Remember what Maya Angelou said about her stories: "I've learned that people will forget what you said, people will forget what you did, but people will never forget how you made them feel." The ability to sense others' motives and feelings grows stronger throughout life and enhances the ability to communicate effectively face to face and via any form of social media.

I am so thrilled Kerry has created this book! When I first coined the term "Senior Entrepreneurship" and launched SeniorEntrepreneurshipWorks.com back in 2012 at the ripe age of 70, Kerry was one of the first people to get it. The aging population is the world's largest, fastest-growing, and most sustainable (we're all living longer) natural resource, and it is virtually untapped. It is redefining the future of work and traditional retirement across all generations, cultures, and geographic boundaries. Experience is a currency, and understanding how to activate and catalyze it across sectors and generations is a new competitive advantage. Until now, most research has been focused on what makes individuals age successfully. Few have asked: How do societies age successfully?

Never Too Old to Get Rich is both a practical hands-on guide to help 50+ individuals translate their entrepreneurial ideas into real businesses and a testament to the ways in which older innovators boost not just their own economic well-being but also their communities', in urban, rural, developed, and developing countries, as well. Creating grassroots entrepreneurial ecosystems is key, but will only happen when different sectors realize the economic impact (what's in it for them) to support this new cohort of entrepreneurs. More financial institutions worldwide, for example, are seeing the numbers of older adults who wish to start businesses as good business for them, too; data is documenting their success rates as proof that this new lending market opportunity exists.

The movement needs books like Kerry's because, as a respected business and financial guru, her advice is authentic and trustworthy. Even more than data and statistics, as a gifted storyteller, she has captured the courage, grit, and resilience of these mid-life entrepreneurs bucking social norms and outdated traditions in real time. And just to be sure they're not seeing opportunity through rose-colored glasses, Kerry ends each tale with a rigorous Q&A to hold their entrepreneurial toes to the fire.

The Experienced Economy is just beginning to gain traction, and we need more out-of-the-box creative, inclusive books like this to strategically support and advance this unprecedented demographic opportunity.

Acknowledgments

Inspired to begin again, to discover a richness to life, to make each day count. That's how I felt as I was interviewing and writing the stories of this remarkable squad of mid-life entrepreneurs.

So I start with a huge thanks to these individuals with all my heart for their time and for sharing their stories with me and with you: Mike Kravinsky, Lazetta Rainey Braxton, Destiny Burns, Mike Foster, Laura Tanner Swinand, Tim Juntgen, Evvy Diamond, Amy Bass, Joan Sadler, Michael Lowe, John Uselton, Paul Tasner, Elena Olivari, Bergen Giordani, Morgen Giordani Reamer, Marvin Gay, Carol Nash, Molly MacDonald, Doug Rauch, Jamal Joseph, Belle Mickelson, Ginny Corbett, Donna Tortorice, Linda LaMagna, Rachel Roth, Joyce Harman, and Michele Meloy Burchfield.

I've been honored to have an illustrious band of colleagues and experts to help me blend these entrepreneurs' stories with practical take-away advice and insight. These experts (many of whom are dear friends as well) whose wisdom I treasure include Elizabeth Isele, Dr. Linda Fried, Paul Irving, Marc Freedman, Cal Halvorsen, Beverly Jones, Gerri Detweiler, Del Gines, BC Clark, David Deeds, Patricia DiVecchio, Rebecca Barnes-Hogg, Ed Rogoff, Maggie Mistal, Rob Lachenauer, Kali McFadden, Bonnie Riggs, Marci Alboher, Kim Eddleston, Linda Abraham, Donna De Carolis, Moira Allen, Sara Sutton, Mary Foley, Pamela Prince-Eason, Nathalie Molina Niño, Sanyin Siang, and Fran Hauser.

My deep appreciation to my agent, Linda Konner, of the Linda Konner Literary Agency, whose savoir faire, publishing insight, and confidence in my work have propelled my mission of empowering individuals to enrich their working lives as well as their personal wealth.

Acknowledgments

My thanks to John Wiley & Sons editor Michael Henton for embracing *Never Too Old to Get Rich* and giving it the green light, as well as chiming in with his vision for a great cover. Gratitude to Purvi Patel, my project editor, and Susan Cerra, Wiley senior production editor, who was the steady sherpa for the assembly of this book. A salute to the Wiley design team, who produced a striking book jacket that exudes the oomph of what readers will find inside including Michael Freeland and Todd Klemme. A special nod to my fine copy editor, James M. Fraleigh, for the care taken with each and every page of this book to make it shine.

Special recognition to Richard Eisenberg, the managing editor of PBS's NextAvenue.org. I always embarrass Rich with my effusive appreciation, but here I go again. Rich, you are one of the sharpest editors I have ever worked with, and, lucky for me, you always make my work shine with your smooth polishing. This time out of the gate, I owe it to you exclusively for precisely shaping this book through your editing and shepherding of the manuscript.

I'm grateful to Twin Cities PBS former president and CEO Jim Pagliarini for his belief in this book and agreeing to co-brand *Never Too Old to Get Rich* via *Next Avenue*, which is produced by Twin Cities PBS for a national audience.

I also would like to send a hearty appreciation to the former director of editorial and content for *Next Avenue*, Shayla Thiel Stern, who was quick to jump on board with enthusiastic support and help garner the backing of Twin Cities PBS.

In addition, *Forbes* editors Janet Novack and Matt Schifrin have regularly contributed their expertise to my work and my understanding of smart ways to share stories of mid-life entrepreneurs and their passions. Janet and Matt, you both know how much I cherish our years of friendship as well.

My thanks to former *Money* magazine editor-in-chief Diane Harris, who has always encouraged and supported me both professionally and personally, and invited me to share stories of passionate entrepreneurs along the way via *Money*.

I would be remiss not to let two of my trusted colleagues on this work and age beat – Christopher Farrell and Mark Miller – know just how much their friendship and help mean to me. Thanks, guys, for being there, and for always making me smile from New York to San Francisco and stops in between.

About the Author

Kerry Hannon is a nationally recognized expert and strategist on career transitions, personal finance, and retirement. She is a frequent TV and radio commentator and is a sought-after keynote speaker at conferences across the country. Kerry focuses on empowering yourself to do more with your career and personal finances – now and for the future.

She has spent more than two decades covering all aspects of careers, business, and personal finance as a columnist, editor, and writer for the nation's leading media companies, including *The New York Times, Forbes, Money, U.S. News & World Report,* and *USA Today.* She has appeared as a career and personal finance expert on *The Dr. Phil Show,* ABC News, CBS, CNBC, *NBC Nightly News,* NPR, and PBS.

Kerry is currently a columnist and regular contributor to *The New York Times,* AARP's Jobs Expert and Great Jobs columnist, a contributing editor and Second Verse columnist at *Forbes,* and the PBS website NextAvenue.org's expert and columnist on personal finance, wealth management, and careers for boomer women.

Kerry is the award-winning author of more than a dozen books, including *Great Jobs for Everyone 50+; Getting the Job You Want After 50 For Dummies; Love Your Job: The New Rules for Career Happiness;* and *What's Next? Finding Your Passion and Your Dream Job in Your Forties, Fifties and Beyond.*

Kerry lives in Washington, D.C., with her husband, documentary producer and editor Cliff Hackel, and her Labrador retriever, Zena.

Follow Kerry on Twitter @KerryHannon, visit her website at KerryHannon.com, and check out her LinkedIn profile at www.linkedin.com/in/kerryhannon.

Introduction

When you think of someone launching a start-up, let's be honest, the image of a twenty-something techie, clad in a hoodie, jeans and fuzzy Allbirds, those sneakerlike shoes made from wool and castor bean oil, springs to mind.

Think again.

Gen Xers and baby boomers are the trendy entrepreneurs, the new risk takers, and though their successful not-so-techie businesses may be under the cool radar, they're on the rise. In *Never Too Old to Get Rich: The Entrepreneur's Guide to Starting a Business Mid-Life*, I'll introduce you to the "kids" on the start-up field and show you how it's done.

Filled with inspiring stories from people who have started their own businesses mid-life, *Never Too Old to Get Rich* is an exciting road map for anyone looking to be their own boss and make their next act building their dream business.

The variety of businesses people are starting in mid-life is amazingly diverse. From a gin distiller to a movie maker to a jewelry designer and a manufacturer of packaging, these in-depth testimonials offer encouragement and advice and prove that it's possible to pursue your passion and build your own successful business at any age. I have interviewed hundreds of older entrepreneurs around the world who are seeking a more fulfilling path. To me, the bottom-line case for why this is such a good idea for older adults is twofold: financial security and, importantly, a personal return.

In this book, you will find:
- Up-to-date resources for launching a business at mid-life
- Snappy profiles of 20 successful older entrepreneurs, describing their inspirational journeys to launching a business or a nonprofit; Q&A conversations; and pull-out boxes containing action steps
- Questions older entrepreneurs must ask before they take the leap to a new venture
- My three-part fitness program: guidelines for becoming financially fit, physically fit, and spiritually fit
- In-depth material on how would-be mid-life entrepreneurs can find capital to start their own business
- Each chapter ends with a recap and your to-do list of action steps

---

There's a way of playing safe, there's a way of using tricks and there's the way I like to play which is dangerously – where you're going to take a chance on making mistakes in order to create something you haven't created before.

– Dave Brubeck, the late American jazz pianist and composer, who was still performing at concert halls around the world at the age of 81, speaking in the PBS documentary Rediscovering Dave Brubeck.

I carry this quote tucked in my wallet to remind me of why I started my own company as a writer, speaker, and consultant when I was in my 40s, and maybe you should, too. It's about fearlessly creating something new ... regardless of your age. It's scary. It's risky. It's hard work, and most entrepreneurs I have ever interviewed have told me that their only regret is that they didn't do it sooner.

More older adults have become entrepreneurs in the last decade than younger people. No kidding. Counterintuitive, right? But it's true. 50+ entrepreneurship is on the rise, and I'll explain why shortly. Being your own boss is no longer a young person's game.

Here's refreshing news for boomers and Gen Xers: when it comes to launching a successful business, youth is not the magic elixir.

"Successful entrepreneurs are middle-aged, not young," according to *Age and High-Growth Entrepreneurship*, a paper by Pierre Azoulay and J. Daniel Kim of the Massachusetts Institute of Technology Sloan School of Management; Benjamin Jones of Northwestern

University's Kellogg School of Management; and Javier Miranda of the Census Bureau's Center for Administrative Records Research.

Most Successful Entrepreneurs: Middle Age and Beyond

"We find that age indeed predicts success, and sharply, but in the opposite way that many observers and investors propose," they wrote. "The highest success rates in entrepreneurship come from founders in middle age and beyond."

The provocative paper may stun some people, but not me. It confirms what I've found studying and interviewing mid-life entrepreneurs for more than a decade; I profiled successful launchers in my book *What's Next?*

Refuting the Conventional Wisdom

Azoulay and coauthors also wrote, "Many observers, and many investors, believe that young people are especially likely to produce the most successful new firms. We use administrative data at the U.S. Census Bureau to study the ages of founders of growth-oriented start-ups in the past decade and find no evidence to suggest that founders in their 20s are especially likely to succeed. Rather, all evidence points to founders being especially successful when starting businesses in middle age or beyond, while young founders appear disadvantaged."

While the authors parsed their research by age, geography, and industry, I was disappointed they didn't tease out data on gender; more on that shortly.

Azoulay and coauthors calculated a mean age of 45 among the 1,700 founders of the fastest-growing new ventures in the past decade. And they found the "batting average" for creating successful firms rises dramatically with age. "A 50-year-old founder is 1.8 times more likely to achieve upper-tail growth than a 30-year-old founder," they wrote.

Older Entrepreneurs versus Younger Ones

As my colleague Richard Eisenberg noted in one of his Next Avenue columns, research from the Kauffman Foundation, a nonpartisan group supporting entrepreneurship, backs the researchers' analysis.

In its 2018 State of Entrepreneurship survey of 2,165 business, Kauffman described how older entrepreneurs reported having less difficulty starting their businesses than younger ones, in a variety of ways.

The authors of *Age and High-Growth Entrepreneurship* theorize that there are a few reasons an older entrepreneur may reap the benefits of start-up success over a younger one: greater management, marketing, and finance experience, and richer, deeper industry knowledge. Also – and this is important – they may have larger financial resources to tap and more social networks to mine for support in leveraging their idea.

The Importance of Work Experience for Successful Ventures

That said, explained Azoulay and coauthors in a *Harvard Business Review* post about the study, "we found that work experience plays a critical role. Relative to founders with no relevant experience, those with at least three years of prior work experience in the same narrow industry as their startup were 85% more likely to launch a highly successful startup."

And there's another study worth noting here. Boomers and Gen Xers – your working world is in for major disturbances between now and 2030, according to a report from the management consulting firm Bain & Company. The depth and breadth of changes in the 2020s will distinguish this transformation from many previous ones, according to the report *Labor 2030: The Collision of Demographics, Automation and Inequality.*

But here's the bigger shock: some of those gyrations will make it *easier* for people in their 50s and 60s to start businesses, the Bain forecasters say. Automation may lower the cost barriers to entrepreneurship. The report notes that "entrepreneurs can use social media postings, targeted search engine ads and email newsletters to launch businesses at a fraction of the marketing budget previously required."

Sorry for the statistic overload, but I have to set the table. Consider this:

- Over the past decade, the highest rate of entrepreneurial activity belongs to the 55-to-64 age group, according to the Kauffman Foundation.

4

- Researchers at the Kauffman Foundation's 2018 State of Entrepreneurship survey of 2,165 business owners found that most older entrepreneurs had support from family and friends to start their businesses, and they were slightly more likely than younger ones to get the encouragement: 82% of those 45+ had support compared with 80% of those under 45.
- Also, older entrepreneurs reported having less difficulty starting their businesses than younger ones, in a variety of ways. For example, while 32% of start-up owners under 45 said obtaining the necessary licenses to operate their business was difficult, only 23% of older ones did. Also, 23% of owners under 45 said registering their business for a state tax ID was difficult, but just 14% of those 45+ felt that way. And 21% of those under 45 said applying for loans was difficult, but a mere 14% of those 45+ did.
- More than half of all U.S. small-business owners are age 50 years and over, according to the U.S. Small Business Administration.
- Older entrepreneurs are more successful: 70% of their start-ups last more than three years, compared with 28% for younger entrepreneurs.
- Approximately 29 million people – two in five Americans ages 50 to 70 – are interested in starting businesses or nonprofit ventures in the next 5 to 10 years, according to research by Encore.org, a nonprofit that promotes second careers focused on improving communities and the world.
- An AARP/Society for Human Resource Management (SHRM) survey of 50+ employed workers shows that 1 in 20 plans to start his or her own business. Nearly one in five older unemployed workers would like to do the same.

We're mostly talking one-person shops that might employ a handful of helpers. And it doesn't always take money, honey. Many small and microbusinesses, particularly freelance, home-based, and online e-commerce businesses, can be launched with under $1,000 in capital.

According to the U.S. Bureau of Labor Statistics, the self-employment rate among workers 65 and older (who don't incorporate) is the highest of any age group in America: 15.5%. In sharp contrast, it's 4.1% for ages 25 to 34.

Importantly, this is not just an American sensation – it's a global movement. Older adults lead about a third of all new firms in Australia and are the fastest-growing segment of entrepreneurs, according to research by Swinburne University of Technology and Queensland University of Technology. Data for older and senior entrepreneurs from 27 European countries found that entrepreneurial activity has taken off in the past five years.

The older generations are the new entrepreneurs, creating employment and driving national productivity, according to research by the London-based Centre for Economics and Business Research. Entrepreneurs over 50 employed more people than start-ups run by younger individuals for the first time in 2016, according to its research. And those over 50 are expected to hold the largest share of the self-employed workforce in the U.K. by 2024.

Older entrepreneurs are brashly stepping into the start-up ethos. Some, admittedly, have been elbowed into opening a business after a corporate downsizing or an early retirement package. Others have been drawn into it by burnout, or the desire to pursue a dream or return to a childhood passion.

With approximately 16% of the world's population 55 years or older and growing, entrepreneurial activity by older adults has economic clout. Across the world, the economic impact of the businesses started and run by older and senior entrepreneurs is massive. These entrepreneurs are creating jobs for themselves and for others; moreover, they contribute billions in tax revenues to government coffers.

The Movement Is Just Getting Underway

Here's why:

- The global 60+ population will encompass more than one in five human beings by mid-century, rising from 900 million in 2015 to 2.1 billion in 2050, according to the World Health Organization.
- In the U.S., people 60 and older will account for 25% of the population by 2030.
- Ten thousand Americans turn 65 each day.

"We've increased our life expectancy by 50% in the last 100 years," says Dr. Linda Fried, dean of Columbia University Mailman School of Public Health. Increased longevity is opening the door for older adults to become an entrepreneurial force. "Society can't afford to lose the assets of older workers: the experience, expertise, commitment, and reliability – and the accumulated knowledge of a lifespan," says Fried.

The Time Has Come

"Population aging represents the world's most compelling business opportunity," says Paul Irving, chairman of the Milken Institute's Center for the Future of Aging. "We are just beginning to see the economic power of older adults – and the wisdom and experience that they bring to the workforce as entrepreneurs."

Today's 60-year-old might reasonably plan to work at least part time for another 15 years, figures Marc Freedman, founder and CEO of Encore.org, and author of *How to Live Forever: The Enduring Power of Connecting the Generations.* "That changes the entire equation about what you want to do, what's possible to do," he says.

Longer lives and fear of outliving their money are motivating many people to keep on keeping on in the working world. The frustrating reality of ageism bias by employers is alive and well, which is why being your own boss has become the default for droves of older workers who are shut out of the workforce by employers who see their expiration date and view them as lacking stamina, up-to-date skills, or perhaps simply being too expensive in terms of salary demands.

What I'm discovering is that people approaching retirement, or already in it, truly want to tap into their skills, knowledge, and experience to create something entrepreneurial, something that is meaningful to them, and an enterprise that makes an impact on the world around us.

And while not everyone is hardwired to work for themselves, those who do choose this path bring decades of experience and networks of contacts they've established over the years. They frequently have other important skills in their wheelhouse, too: a firm work ethic, management know-how, and often, better access to capital.

While each new business owner takes a unique path, I have found there's a common spine that those who succeed share. Many entrepreneurs at this stage of life are spurred into action after experiencing a life catastrophe, perhaps a health issue of their own, or someone close to them dying young. For a more in-depth look at this phenomenon, I encourage you to read my colleague and friend Mark Miller's excellent book, *Jolt: Stories of Trauma and Transformation*. A world event may have rocked them in a way that made them pause and think, is this what it is all about? Is this the work I was put in this world to do? "One of the most striking things I learned writing the book is that people who have experienced jolts regard their trauma as a very profound, valuable gift," Miller told me. "The essential 'gift' is that trauma shakes everything up – our expectations for the future, our values, and how we want to spend our time. That opens the door to change."

Those who succeed typically set a flexible time horizon for their venture. They don't make any rash moves. If necessary, they add the vital skills and degrees before they make the leap. They often apprentice or volunteer beforehand. But at the heart of all of their efforts lies a yearning to make a difference in the world, or to pursue a dream, or hone a hobby, to *live*.

They reach out to their networks of social and professional contacts to ask for help and guidance. They downsize and plan their financial lives so they can afford a cut in pay or the cost of a start-up. Several are fortunate to have a spouse's steady income or some outside investments, retirement savings, or pensions in place to ease the transition to their new line of work.

Different flavors of ice cream, as my sister, Pat, likes to say. Some start-ups have big grand schemes and will require long hours, hard work, and serious capital infusions. Others can be more organic, such as a consulting business or a one-woman craft shop on Etsy, that embrace a part-time, flexible work schedule.

In *Never Too Old to Get Rich*, you will discover examples of both pathways.

In my reporting and consulting with hundreds of individuals about entrepreneurship over the past few years, I've been inspired by the innovation, grit, and possibilities that today's older entrepreneurs represent.

Entrepreneurship among those in mid-life has two other noteworthy impacts. First, studies show that older people who remain engaged in work are physically and mentally healthier. Second, data from Finland shows a positive relationship between later-life start-ups and positive self-perception of one's aging.

Bottom line: being the boss feels good.

I'm not going to sugarcoat it. It's not for the faint of heart, and it takes time to lay a stable foundation to make it, well, work.

"Entrepreneurship is a precarious line of work," Cal J. Halvorsen, a noted retirement researcher and assistant professor at the Boston College School of Social Work, told me when I ran into him at the Gerontological Society of America conference in Boston and shared with him the title of this book. "Those who have higher levels of assets, spouses who have steady jobs, or families with a modicum of wealth are in a better place to start a business. If their ventures fail, they have something to fall back on. Know that entrepreneurship can be a high-risk, high-reward game. Do your homework."

Halvorsen doesn't want people to think he's all gloom and doom about second-act entrepreneurship, though. "It can be so exciting," he noted.

Older entrepreneurs, Halvorsen said, "gain a whole lot of flexibility in their work, and that's a major motivating driver for a lot of people. That does become more important the older you are. And they gain autonomy; they get to become their own boss."

The people who are best prepared to become entrepreneurs, Halvorsen said, are those who have "higher levels of human capital, social capital, and financial capital."

I asked him to explain. "Human capital might be, for example, education and work experience. Social capital would be their social network. Financial capital would be their financial assets and wealth. If you have higher levels of these, it has been shown that you can be more successful in entrepreneurship."

Fortunately, these forms of capital tend to increase with age, because you have had more time to cultivate them. As a result, older people in general would likely be more successful at entrepreneurship than younger ones, Halvorsen said.

I get it, and Halvorsen's advice is worth noting.

That said, many mid-life entrepreneurs – and, I suspect, you, if you're reading this book – do have the right experience, resilience, and resources to be successful, and have fun too.

Never Too Old to Get Rich is divided into four parts: Turning a Passion into a Business, Building a Winning Senior-Junior Partnership, The Path to Social Entrepreneurship, and Winning Strategies of Female Entrepreneurs.

How to Use This Book

I have designed *Never Too Old to Get Rich* to show you how to make the best moves right now to start your own business. In these pages, you'll discover the ultimate guide to making your venture a successful one. I'll give you the action steps to take to launch. I'll deliver the professional advice and strategies I've been doling out as a career transition, retirement, and personal finance expert and journalist for more than three decades. Each chapter will conclude with a short recap and action steps to keep you working toward your goals.

Here are a few suggestions to consider before we start:

- Take a breath. This is not a leap into the abyss of the unknown. Entrepreneurship is a process.
- Soul-search. You will want to begin with a solid MRI of your own passion and personality, talents and inner drive to start a business. The big questions: Why start this business? Why you? And why now?
- Prepare to get your hands dirty to discover just what it will take to make your dream a reality. That means picking up the phone to ask for help, researching, and getting under the hood of what it will take to really do this in terms of time and money.
- Get fit: It's essential to be physically fit, financially fit, and spiritually fit to face the stress and demands that will lie ahead.

I wrote this book to help you be your own boss – in fact, to help you be your own *best* boss. It's time to find joy in your work life and follow those dreams you harbor. It's a decision I've never regretted, and I want to help you feel the same way, too. And in full disclosure, the title of this book, *Never Too Old to Get Rich*, is a tease in a way. It does bring to mind the financial rewards that are without question a huge motivation for starting a business. And that is my hope for you. But while I am a dreamer, the title has another meaning for me, and, hopefully, for you too.

Getting rich can, and should, be also about the inner richness that comes from creating a new product or service that changes lives and our world and gives back. It's the richness of doing work we love, alongside people we respect. It's the powerful rich reward of taking a risk, trying something that scares you, learning new things, meeting different people, achieving personal goals.

All of which may have nothing at all to do with the size of your bank account. But you're rich in ways that are intangible and that matter deeply in this journey of life. It just depends on your definition of wealth.

Let's buckle up and enjoy the ride!

ALSO BY KERRY HANNON

Great Jobs for Everyone 50+, Updated Edition: Finding Work That Keeps You Happy and Healthy … and Pays the Bills

Getting the Job You Want After 50 for Dummies

Love Your Job: The New Rules for Career Happiness

Great Jobs for Everyone 50+: Finding Work That Keeps You Happy and Healthy … and Pays the Bills

Suddenly Single: Money Skills for Divorcees and Widows

PART

TURNING A PASSION INTO A BUSINESS

Transforming a passion into paying work can do a number on your desire for it, so you need to plan ahead and test the waters with care.

Before you step out on this path, be clear about the role that this passion, or hobby, plays in your life right now. For many of us, the things that stir up the most passion – and we always wish we could just have more time to do them – are not anchored in the world of commerce. In fact, the time spent devoted to them is quite frankly our respite from our hectic working lives and family demands. It's where we go to clear our minds and quiet anxiety.

Tapping into that well of renewal to produce an income can turn it upside down. I'm wildly passionate about horses, for example. I fantasize about what it would be like to truly devote all my time and energy to this world. When someone asks, "What would you do if you didn't need the money?" I would say, spend my time riding and surround myself with horses and dogs.

But I know in my heart that a career training and working with horses would never be a good fit for me. It's my special place to escape and breathe, far away from world of deadlines and travel, and yes, people. If the barn became my office, I would lose that enchanted world that has bewitched me since the age of six.

Another example is a friend of mine who is a talented gardener. She decided to open a landscape design business when she took an early retirement package from her law firm. But she soon realized when her garden time was every day and the long hours were mostly spent alone, she had made a big mistake. She was lonely and miserable. You see, her garden was her respite from her hectic life. When it *was* her life, she missed the people connection – the energy she got from interacting with her social work – and it lost its magic.

So, beware of ruining your hobby. To take this route, you must be absolutely certain you do have the talent and the willingness to shift your mindset to make it succeed.

In the following eight chapters, you will meet entrepreneurs who have taken that calculated risk and blend earning a paycheck with their passion – and they'll share their lessons learned along the way.

Lights, Camera, Action

Mike Kravinsky, Nextnik Films, LLC
Courtesy of Sali Dimond.

W hen Mike Kravinsky went to work as a video editor at ABC News in 1981, he figured he would spend a year there and then head out to Los Angeles to become a filmmaker.

Well, it didn't quite work out that way. Over the course of 29 years, he worked as an editor and technical director for news broadcasts like *World News Tonight* and *Good Morning America*, and news magazine shows like *20/20* and *Primetime Live*.

"ABC turned out to be a great place to work," Kravinsky says. "They gave me great opportunities and experiences and one thing led to another." But then the day came when the jig was up. He accepted a buyout. "I was ready," he says. "It had become routine."

After retiring in 2010, the 65-year-old is now following his dream to be a filmmaker once again, although he's not in Hollywood, but Arlington, Virginia. His independent film company: Nextnik Films, LLC.

From the start of his transition, Kravinsky had his wife, Liza, a composer, urging him to "do what makes you happy." And the couple, who have no children, has a knack for living frugally. "We're not living on peanut butter and jelly sandwiches, but we do drive a 12-year old car, and we don't buy expensive clothes and furniture. It's just our lifestyle," he says.

Nonetheless, one of his first moves was to tap an adviser at a no-load mutual fund company for some guidance. He wanted to be sure he was making good choices with the funds he had accumulated in his former employer's retirement plan, and, of course, to sort out how to manage his buyout monies.

And since he was not exactly certain of his new direction initially, Kravinsky spent time working on his website, which was focused on articles about change and transition, that he had launched before he took the buyout. "I had wanted an outlet to do some writing and videos, and talk to people who had taken professional leaps of faith," he recalls.

Once on his own, and with the website up and running, he started a blog. Kravinsky soon realized, however, that he was doing the same thing he had always done. His magazine-style video and online stories about career changers were all newsy.

"I should get out of my comfort zone here," he told himself. "Why don't I create a character, based on what I am experiencing, as well as what those people who I had done stories about had gone through. So that's where the first film was born," he says.

It began in stages. First, a 30-minute Web series. Then Kravinsky got the urge to push beyond. He spent two months adding and rewriting scenes, and went back and filmed to build his series into the 77-minute feature film.

That film, *The Nextnik*, is the story of a worker who has been downsized after 25 years without warning and must reinvent himself. It sounds a tad autobiographical, and, of course, it is in a way. The story revolves around him searching for something new and experimenting with different careers.

Kravinsky has now completed three feature films and is writing his fourth. His films, *The Nextnik* (2013), *Geographically Desirable* (2015), and *Nothing to Do* (2017), have won accolades at independent film festivals across the country and are steadily sending income his way through streaming fees when viewed on Amazon Prime.

The first film cost $25,000 to make, "which is like nothing," says Kravinsky. Those funds were mostly earmarked for actors and crew salaries. "These films are at the low-end of ultra-low budgets," he says with a laugh.

The financing for the first two films came from an inheritance of $90,000. The last one, *Nothing To Do*, was financed by a combination of savings and money earned from *Geographically Desirable*. His second and third films are both available on Amazon. "Amazon is now doing for small independent filmmakers what they originally did for authors who self-publish," Kravinsky says. "It's treated as any other film on their platform. The goal, like books, is to develop an audience for your work."

Does he make money? "Yes," he says. Will he profit from his films? "I don't know," he says. "I get thousands of daily watched minutes on Amazon Prime with *Geo Desire*, and it's making a decent return. *Nothing To Do* is gaining traction."

Building a successful film business takes passion and a smattering of pixie dust. "Filmmaking is art," Kravinsky says. "Like music, books, paintings, photography, et cetera. I hope to pay off the investment and get into the black, but it's art. It's speculative. If I make a lot of money, excellent. If I don't, that's the business. That's where I'm at."

Kravinsky is realistic. "I have a set amount of money to spend. If I spend it and don't get enough of a return, I hope the experience will get me jobs on the creative work of others in the future. I don't jeopardize my retirement saving," he says.

One cost-saving advantage he has is that he is willing to tap his own sweat equity for his films. He auditions and hires actors. He hires technical people – a director of photography and a makeup artist – but the rest he does himself: the writing, producing, directing, and postproduction. He secures the locations to shoot in the Washington, D.C. area: Arlington, Fairfax, and Leesburg in Virginia, and Rehoboth Beach, Delaware. "I'm the one directing people and ordering food at the same time," Kravinsky laughs.

As for his Hollywood dream? "Of course, it would be great to be nominated for an Academy Award down the road, but you know what, if I can just make movies and make a little money doing it, I am going to be really happy," he says. That's rich.

Making It Work

I asked Mike to look back and share his thoughts on his shift to starting his own independent film company.

Kerry: What did starting your own business mean to you personally?

Mike: Freedom. There's something nice about routine, but routine can really start wearing on you when there's really nothing left to accomplish. I now have the freedom to take on projects and execute them in my own vision – essentially being my own boss in a creative venture. Each film that I do is like starting a new business. It is like a new crew, new actors, new locations. I really enjoyed my career in TV news, but it was time. For me, making my own fictional films seemed like the right thing.

Were you confident that you were doing the right thing? Any second-guessing?

I was absolutely confident that I was doing the right thing. Not necessarily the website and blog, but I knew I was doing the right thing by moving on. It really felt good when I was initially doing the blog after I left ABC. But there was something gnawing that I wasn't accomplishing everything that I wanted to do. Basically I have been living something that I thought I would do in my 20s – move out to L.A. and become a filmmaker. This was the time to take a chance and the technology was such I could afford it.

I didn't have any doubts about leaving ABC. It was time. But I did have a lot of second thoughts about how I should approach my next act. I knew I wanted to continue to make media, but the question was should I make documentaries, narratives, shorts, feature length? A video blog? I needed to find what got me up in the morning. Financially, I thought if it all came crashing down, I could go back to the news business as a freelance editor because the gig economy is pretty big right now. I felt it could be a fallback.

Anything you would have done differently?

The little misdirection I might have taken really brought me to where I am. I would have had to do the blog to realize I was doing the same thing that I did at ABC and remind myself … wait a minute, I can make movies now. That process gave me the idea to do the movie.

The biggest mistake I made was rushing. In search of what I wanted to try next. I didn't have a real plan before I left ABC, which is exactly what you say you should not do.

When I decided to try my hand at filmmaking I wanted to make my first film fast. I should have slowed down some and enjoyed the journey more.

It would have been better for me if I had started off on small films. I enjoyed doing them. But I would have concentrated on short films first if I had to do it over again. And the writing is always challenging.

How do you measure your success?

I would measure my success by making a little bit of money. It's really nice to get people happy about your product and want to discuss it. I'm not looking to become wealthy, but I am looking to make a product and be able to sell it.

Importantly, success for me is touching people emotionally. Of course, I want to make money. Filmmaking is a business. I have learned if you are true to yourself in your writing and directing people and enjoy your work, hopefully the money will come.

How big a role did financial rewards play in your decision to make a transition?

Financial rewards did not play a huge role. I was fortunate enough to be with an organization, Disney ABC, that provided us with a comfortable retirement plan, 401(k) and all that stuff.

For most, the arts aren't big moneymakers, particularly if you are creating something fresh. I knew that going in, and I was just ready. My feeling was if I got into any kind of trouble financially, I knew that I could go back and do some freelance. As long as we don't go crazy and buy a Tesla everything will work out.

I have been able to keep costs down because I do pretty much everything that I can do. I write it, edit it, direct it. My wife is the composer. Even my dog plays a role.

One way I can make money today on my films today is through Amazon Prime per-view streaming fees. My hope is to make enough money to continue to make films.

How did your preparation help you succeed?

The preparation was working behind the camera on the blog videos and then the Web series. Working in TV prepared me to be very exacting in my preparation of a production. But what was missing from my years in television was an understanding of emotion.

Although much of what I learned creatively, technically and running on deadlines on shows like *Good Morning America, Primetime Live,* and *20/20* [was] movable to narrative films, there was still a significant learning curve to go from reality to fiction, and I honestly continue to learn with each production.

My career, a couple of things helped. One is the technical. I worked with the top video professionals at ABC; as a result I have a solid understanding of the technical and creative side of news editing. Transferring that to fictional films took some work. The way a fictional film is paced. How the story unfolds is much different than news, so there was and is a big learning curve there. The other thing is dealing with people.

At ABC, I was a technical director, where I was crew chief for as many as 25 people on a television show. Now I am dealing with personalities and creative people.

What do you tell people who ask you for advice on starting a business?

You can't just do it. Everybody's situation is different. There are financial issues. There are family issues. What if you have a sick parent or kids in school? Some people just financially cannot do it. If you're in a position that you are able to do it, and you have some savings, then you can give it a shot. You should have a year of savings backlogged, so you are able to go back to school to learn something new if you have to, or work part time in a particular industry.

The biggest preparation is you have to feel financially comfortable in whatever it is you're going to start to do. Do the downsizing and whatever you need to do to be able to take on something new. Then hopefully your new work will start paying some kind of salary. It might not be much to start, but enough to pay the bills. That's really the bottom line.

Look at the end product. Enjoy the journey. Don't stress. I know that is very simplistic advice particularly if it is your own money.

Finally, don't rush. Enjoy the ride. Write about things you know about and are passionate about. Don't write things that include specific locations and things you need to get. Look around your house, look at your friends and things you have free access to. Then write a story with all of those things. That is the reason our dog Charlie is in every one of my films. She does it for the little hunks of cheese.

What books did you find helpful?

Your book, *What's Next? Follow Your Passion and Find Your Dream Job*, and Marc Freedman's *The Big Shift*. He's something of a pragmatist. You have to be very pragmatic.

A big source for me for what I do is YouTube interviews with writers and editors about their craft. I like TED Talks.

Any unexpected surprises?

I didn't think about the business of filmmaking. You have to sell your product – to get people's attention. That's all new for me. They're not going to be beating down your doors. You have to get buzz.

What are some of the unexpected rewards and surprises?

The most unexpected surprise about the last film at all of the festivals was how it touched people. We all ended up getting into some very personal discussions with festival goers about how they dealt with an aging parent and how dealing with the end of a mother or father's life and how it affected them. It was beautiful and amazing to have a total stranger want to discuss a personal time in their lives. That is what art is all about. Moving people, touching people emotionally.

What was the biggest challenge?

Writing was the biggest challenge. It is hard to create a world that seems real, but is fiction.

10 TIPS FOR MID-CAREER ENTREPRENEURS

I asked my friend and one of the best career coaches I know, Beverly Jones, author of *Think Like an Entrepreneur, Act Like a CEO* for her tips for budding entrepreneurs. Jones has a great perspective on this topic since she has lived it herself.

In 1999, after more than two decades as a top corporate lawyer and lobbyist, she took a golden parachute retirement package from her position as vice president of external affairs and policy at Consolidated Natural Gas. She was 53.

Jones had an inkling of what path she'd like to follow. She had always enjoyed mentoring others and had done so throughout her entire career. So it was a natural shift to find a way to take this innate ability and redirect it to create a business where she could help people navigate their work lives and get paid for it.

She was fortunate to have a modest pension, which gave her some flexibility about how fast she needed to ramp up her venture. To stay engaged and make some income, she initially did some legal work for a law firm in Washington, D.C., as well as some lobbying for a nonprofit.

Then to add the credentials she needed to enter the new field, she went back to school to obtain a Leadership Coaching Certificate from Georgetown University. But she didn't stop there. She attended coaching workshops, hired her own career coach, and read extensively about the field and related areas such as self-help, spirituality, and fitness. "In time, I began to find my own voice as a coach and felt confident I was doing what I was meant to do," Jones says.

Among her coaching clients at her Clearways Consulting (clearwaysconsulting.com), based in Washington, D.C., are attorneys, business owners, and high-level government workers (and the occasional friend pro bono) – many of them mid-life looking for their "what's next."

Here are Jones's top tips for those looking to launch their own business.

1. **Be clear about your goals**. You probably have more than one reason for starting a business. Sure, you want to earn some money. But are you also aching for more variety? Do you dream of a career that allows a more flexible lifestyle? Or do you want to take the next step with a hobby you already love? Write down what you hope to achieve, frame specific goals, and remember that your bottom line is just one way to measure your progress.

2. **Start early to prepare**. If launching your own business is something you want to do "some day," it is never too soon to start laying groundwork. If running your business will require a new set of skills, you might build expertise through local or online college courses. Or perhaps you could start a small side gig, to test your business idea and get some experience. At the same time, do what it takes to get your life in order. This could mean paying off debt and building a nest egg, committing to a fitness program so that you're in good shape to work, or creating habits that will help you be more organized.

3. **Learn business basics**. From choosing a legal structure to paying your taxes, you must comply with laws. The rules that apply will depend on the state where you live, the nature of your activities, and the kind of entity you create. And, even when you have a small-business accountant, it is vital that you know how to measure your costs, keep track of expenses, and decide what to charge. You can take courses, work for a spell in a small business, or apply to a business incubator, as you learn what it takes to run a company.

4. **Build your network**. As you grow as an entrepreneur, your network will be a critical asset. You can visualize it as a complex pattern of human relationships, spreading out around you in concentric circles. While the innermost ring may include close friends and family, further out are

(Continued)

10 TIPS FOR MID-CAREER ENTREPRENEURS (*Cont'd*)

people you know only slightly, like alumni of your college, members of your clubs, and folks who live nearby. Everyone matters. Even your most casual contacts can support your success. Throughout your expanding network are potential mentors, collaborators, customers, and fans.

5. **Surround yourself with positive people**. As entrepreneurs, you must deal with discouraging moments. False starts, rejected proposals, and disinterested audiences are part of the game. Because emotions are contagious, one way to protect yourself from some of that negativity is to stay in touch with upbeat people. Try to reach out to the optimists in your circle, and avoid the complainers who leave you feeling down. And find other ways to surround yourself with positive voices, like reading uplifting books or finding community events that leave you feeling good.

6. **Offer and seek help**. Even though you know that connectivity is the lifeblood of small business, building a supportive community can be a challenge. A starting point is to look for opportunities to be helpful. Reach out to old friends and new acquaintances, listen to their problems, and look for small ways to offer assistance. Introduce folks with good reasons to meet each other. Support other small businesses. And give authentic praise. The more comfortable you feel as a helper, the easier it will be to ask for the support and encouragement you need.

7. **Create a social media strategy**. Even if you avoid Facebook and other apps in your personal life, don't ignore the power that social media can bring to your business. A smart mix of channels can help you check out the competition, understand your potential customers, keep up with industry news, and show off your products. It takes a while to get a feel for tools like Twitter, LinkedIn, and Pinterest, so practice using them as you expand your network.

8. **Define and promote your brand**. Your brand sets you apart from the competition. As an entrepreneur, you will need to identify your special value, and have a plan for spreading the word. To get comfortable with projecting your unique strengths, a useful exercise is to write a brief statement summarizing your *personal* brand. Be honest with yourself about how you want others to see you. And your current brand can help pave the way for your future business. For example, if you dream of opening a doggie day care facility, your brand might include your skill as a dog trainer. You can raise your brand profile by connecting with dog lovers, whether that means posting on Twitter or volunteering with service organizations.

9. **Listen to your customers**. Turning yourself into an entrepreneur may require a shift in your mindset. When you start your business, your customers will ultimately determine whether you succeed. So now, wherever

you are in your career, cultivate the habit of listening intently to the people who are impacted by your work, including your boss and your colleagues. Make it your job to understand what your "customers" need, what they want, and what they think. And keep looking for new projects and products that might help your "customers" meet their goals.

10. **Learn to be motivated.** You may have heard that "entrepreneurs are passionate about their work." But what if you're not sure you can maintain that kind of passion? The reality is that motivation is something you *can* acquire and manage. Now, in your current job, you can develop the skill of triggering your own drive and enthusiasm. One way to build motivation is by setting small goals, taking action, and experiencing moments of success. If you have put off tackling an important project, schedule an hour to focus on it exclusively. Quickly create a list of small subtasks and power through them for the 60 minutes. By actually getting some things done, you will motivate yourself to do even more on the project tomorrow.

HANNON'S THREE-PART FITNESS PROGRAM

Become financially fit. Find ways to get lean and mean. If you're financially fit, possibilities open for you to try new things and shift into new areas of work. Debt is a dream killer. The biggest stumbling block for many mid-life entrepreneurs is money. Do a budget. Where can you trim expenses? Adjust your spending to a stricter budget. Pay down debts. Downsize your home, perhaps. This can take time, but it's critical. You may not be able to take a salary from your new venture initially, so savings socked away to tap and an emergency fund are essential ingredients to your eventual success.

Become physically fit. I don't mean running fast miles or bench-pressing, but walk a mile or two regularly, swim a few times a week perhaps. Eat nutritiously. When you're fit, you bring positivity to your work and your life. It gives you the stamina and energy you will need to face new challenges. You'll be mentally sharper, feel good, and a can-do attitude emerges. People will want to be around you and work with you.

Become spiritually fit. I don't mean a religious practice per se. Starting your own business is demanding. Find a place to center yourself, and de-stress. You will draw strength from having a ballast, a core of calmness, as you head down this path. You might practice yoga, tai chi, or meditation, or walk your dog along quiet pathways, as I do.

Shape Your Network

I can't overemphasize the importance of networking to help your business get off the ground and grow. As I like to say, networking is one letter away from *not* working. And it rings true. Your network, your tribe, your believers are the ones who are going to propel you forward to success.

Shift slowly. Prepare for a change. Look where you want to shift. Network with people doing those jobs. Ask how they got there, how they do their jobs, what they love about it. People love to talk about themselves and their work.

Connect with a mentor. Who do you know to chaperone you along your new path? Arrange to meet with your mentor, either in person or online, to help you learn the ropes. If you are in the exploring stage, you might start your exploration with a virtual mentor. Your local Rotary Club or chamber of commerce can be a wonderful source of mentors and advisers.

One of my favorite sources is PivotPlanet (PivotPlanet.com), a service that connects people with expert advisers working in hundreds of professions for affordable one-on-one, one-hour videoconference, phone, or in-person sessions. Most one-hour sessions range from $40 to $125. You might also reach out to a start-up coach, such as Jeff Williams at Bizstarters.com, who works with "aspiring business owners" over age 50. You can tap into podcasts and videos on his website aimed at newbies.

Be specific about what help you need. When you do identify someone you want to reach out to, be specific about your goals for the connection. Write them down in your journal to help you focus on what you hope to achieve. You might have a certain business task at hand, something as simple as wanting to give you advice on how to spruce up your image, such as proper attire. It could be someone who can guide you on the best way to price your product or service. Or perhaps you're looking for someone who can introduce you to some of the players in the market. Don't rule out a mentor younger than you, who can offer more experience and direction when it comes to areas like technology or social media where you might not feel quite as confident.

Comb your circle of friends, family, and business colleagues. Tap into LinkedIn and Facebook contacts who are running their own businesses for direction on how they got started and more.

Invest in additional education and training. Add skills and certificates. It doesn't have to be a full-blown degree program. Start with one or two classes. Invest in additional education and training. Research the skills, diplomas, or even degrees required for your new business. Add the essential expertise before you make the leap, and if you can, do it part time while you're still employed in career number one. Startupinstitute.com, for example, offers courses on upping your sales expertise and digital marketing.

Cruise the web. Check out StartupNation.com, a site dedicated to small-business group and community forums. Tap into entrepreneurship resources at EIX.org. If you're seeking an encore venture focused on social impact, visit Encore.org (encore.org/for-encore-seekers) for resources to help you get started.

Be a bookworm. Pick up copies of my books, *What's Next?* or *Great Jobs for Everyone 50+.* (I couldn't resist a plug.) Encore.org's vice president Marci Alboher's *The Encore Career Handbook,* Chris Farrell's *Purpose and a Paycheck: Finding Meaning, Money, and Happiness in the Second Half of Life,* John Tarnoff's *Boomer Reinvention: How to Create Your Dream Career Over 50,* and Nancy Collamer's *Second-Act Careers: 50+ Ways to Profit from Your Passions During Semi-retirement* are must-reads for great ideas and inspiration.

Volunteer. I also recommend doubling down your networking efforts in any associations or organizations devoted to your passion or hobby. Get involved and volunteer. Attend meetings. You never know who you might meet who can give you invaluable assistance while you research starting your own hobby-based business. Meantime, keep in mind, these may be the people who in time are your ultimate customers. This is your clan.

Reach out to your alumni network. You never know who can bring you clients or help you build your business via an alumni association at your college or university, or even an alumni group at one of your former employers. Your alma mater's career service center very well may have resources devoted to mid-life entrepreneurs such as an incubator on campus, or continuing education classes geared toward career changers and entrepreneurs that are offered online, or via weekend workshops. You might even be able to make a connection to access current students who can lend a hand.

Don't ignore the big players in the small-business help arena. Your local Rotary Club or chamber of commerce can be a wonderful source of mentors and advisers. Find a local chapter of SCORE (score.org), a nonprofit association devoted to teaching entrepreneurs the ins and outs of getting underway. SCORE is a resource partner with the U.S. Small Business Administration (SBA). The organization, founded in 1954, is headquartered in Herndon, Virginia, and Washington, D.C., and has around 300 chapters throughout the United States and its territories, with more than 10,000 volunteer mentors nationwide. Both working and retired executives and business owners donate time and expertise as business counselors. SCORE mentors will advise you for free, in person or online. Seek out a local Small Business Development Center (americassbdc.org).

Be prepared for setbacks. Starting a new business takes time and can feel like a bit of a roller coaster, even when it's an area you know well from years of being a customer or a participant. It might take off zooming, but chances are there will be blips along the way in the early days. It's easy to be discouraged, but that's when a solid mentor by your side comes in handy.

Chapter Recap

In this chapter, we learned that patience is a key to letting your business plan unfold. We reviewed the importance of being fit financially, physically, and spiritually as a core blueprint for success. Sometimes the path to starting your own enterprise only emerges over a period of time. You need to allow yourself the space for discovery, and you must be willing to set limits on just how much of your own capital you are willing to commit to your venture. There's a line between starting a vanity business and truly engaging in an entrepreneurial venture that has the potential to have both personal *and* financial rewards. Last, you must be pragmatic in order not to blow through your savings and risk your future financial security.

YOUR TO-DO LIST

- Begin a journal in a notebook or computer file for your "Be My Own Boss" program.
- In your journal, write your professional and personal goals for your own potential business.
- Do some brainstorming and create a list of the types of businesses that might be possible for you to launch that revolve in the orbit of your passion or hobby. Hint: For me, with my equine preoccupation, it might be to open a tack shop

that sells equipment, clothing, and supplies; start a riding lesson business; write books and expert columns and newsletters; or even launch a start-up equestrian magazine in my niche.
- Make a list of people you know who have started businesses from their passion or hobby, and then reach out and ask them what their challenges were, how they handled setbacks, and for advice.
- Write down in your journal your goals for working with a mentor to help you focus on what you hope to achieve.
- Start Kerry's fitness program. Set up a routine exercise program. Do a budget. Take a class in mindfulness or meditation.

CHAPTER

Money Maven

Lazetta Rainey Braxton, Financial Fountains

"A dollar within our household always had a purpose that was already marked," says Lazetta Rainey Braxton, 45, a Certified Financial Planner (CFP), founder of Financial Fountains (financialfountains.com), a fee-only financial planning and registered investment advisory firm based in Baltimore, Maryland, chair of the Association of African American Financial Advisors (AAAA), and president of the AAAA Foundation.

"I received my first paycheck when I was 16 from the Golden Corral restaurant, where I worked as a hostess," Braxton says. "For the first time, the money was all *mine,* and I felt a weight of what to do with it. What did I want to earmark it for?"

Braxton grew up in the small rural town of South Hill, Virginia, and money was stretched in her family. Her mother and father both worked full time – a factory worker and construction worker, respectively – but they often had to go into debt to make ends meet. "My parents didn't go to college," she says. "Their jobs didn't earn a lot of money, but in many ways, they struggled with money because of lack of access to basic personal financial concepts."

Her passion for learning about finance and helping people, particularly African American families like her own, with financial planning was driven by watching her parents grapple with money. "At the time, I didn't know I was going to make a career out of it, but this was personal to me and I knew I was going to ultimately teach people how to manage their money," she says.

While Braxton knew she had her parents' love, if she was going to go to college, she would need to pay her own way. "I had financial responsibility very early," she says. "If I needed anything, or wanted anything, I had to figure it out myself. My parents were extremely supportive, but I knew there was a lot of financial stress in the household."

So she worked two jobs throughout her high school and college years to stash away funds to pay tuition. She graduated from the University of Virginia, earning a degree in finance and international business, in 1995. "I worked hard before and during college to earn enough for my tuition – it was an investment in my future," she says. "That was my first investment in *me*."

After graduation, she added skills and experience, and honed her vision. She held management and executive positions in the corporate and banking arenas with employers such as Marriott, Wachovia Asset Management, and Diversified Trust Company. She added an MBA from Wake Forest University and a CFP certificate before opening her own business as a registered investment adviser in 2008.

Bringing Empathy to the Client's Table

"I bring a strong sense of empathy to clients of color from difficult financial backgrounds," Braxton says. "And I can offer personalized financial planning, investment management, and educational seminars to those individuals, families, businesses and institutions from around the country."

Her planning services are filling a gap. The financial planning profession has a big problem: fewer than 3.5% of all the 80,000 CFPs in the U.S. are black or Latino – just 2,700.

Braxton's initial start-up costs, around $10,000, were earmarked for computer equipment and legal counsel for compliance requirements. Braxton's a one-woman show and prefers to work virtually via Zoom, which keeps down the cost of overhead for fancy office space.

She tapped personal savings in nonretirement accounts for funding. Braxton and her husband, Brad, a theologian, opted years earlier to live off one income, so the couple had reserves set aside.

Braxton's mission: "to bring personal finance to people like my own parents and to younger investors just starting out who don't have a high net worth," she says. Most of her clients have household incomes that range from a modest $75,000 to around $400,000. About half of her clients are African American and cover a wide age span, from 22 to 90.

"I work with many people who feel they're unworthy for a planner because they don't have enough assets," she says. "My aim is to give them courage and wisdom to understand that they can create wealth, which gives them options to do what they're supposed to do on this earth."

Braxton has built a practice that is especially welcoming for younger women. It's a passion for her stemming for her own childhood where money was tight.

The fact is most younger women don't discuss financial matters. There's a social taboo for women of all ages around talking about money.

That's a problem when you consider the future scenario for many women. Women typically live longer than men – 81 years versus 76 years – according to statistics from the U.S. Department of Health and Human Services. "Living longer means you need more money for the extra years of living and healthcare, and that creates serious problems for women – many who are divorced or widowed at older ages," says Cindy Hounsell, the founder and president of WISER – the Women's Institute for a Secure

Retirement – a nonprofit organization dedicated to women's financial education and advocacy.

Automating savings from a young age can help – even $25 per pay period, says Braxton. "It seems like nothing, but it's the habit," she says. "It's not the dollar amount. Once they get going they see they can do that, and they can up it to $50, then to $100. It's not hoping that someone will do that for you later in life. It's self-care. You have to value yourself first. It will dictate your future financial well-being."

Negotiating for higher pay can also make a big difference in the amount young women can set aside for retirement. "I am encouraged by what I see," Braxton says. "I encourage the 20-somethings who have sought me out for help to negotiate as much as they can for salary because more money means more resources all the way around for the rest of their lives."

Developing a contract side gig through an online freelance marketplace such as Upwork or Fiverr, or selling craft items on eBay or Etsy, "is a great way to have an incremental pot on the side to use for savings," Braxton says.

And she gives similar advice to her clients at the other end of the spectrum who are nearing retirement. Some people have always worked a variety of jobs in retirement, but for a growing number of retirees, it is now a necessity. "With my clients, I'm having retirement discussions about transitioning their lifestyle gradually," she says. "We talk about ways that their skill set allows them to be a part of the gig economy, and if they need to add any new skills to stay relevant in the work force and how to budget for that cost."

Even for those who have saved enough to retire comfortably, working for pay in retirement can help provide a safety net and peace of mind. It helps people put off dipping into retirement accounts and may even allow some to continue contributing to their retirement savings.

The pay can also help provide a cushion to allow someone to delay tapping into Social Security until age 70, which increases annual Social Security income by nearly 8% compared with retiring at the full retirement age. The income can also help with medical bills not covered by Medicare.

Making It Work

I asked Lazetta to look back and share her thoughts on her shift to starting her own financial planning business.

> **Kerry: What did starting your own business mean to you personally?**

Lazetta: My vision is to provide access to financial planning for those overlooked and underserved by Wall Street. So many people thought you need to be wealthy to work with a financial adviser. But I am saying it is affordable.

> **Were you confident that you were doing the right thing? Any second-guessing?**

Absolutely, I was confident that I was doing the right thing – now, how I was going to materialize this vision, I had no clue. I continue to make it up as I go along. I felt the pain looking at my parents' situation. I feel I was called to this earth and it just stayed on my conscience all through my life helping people with their finances, even when I was younger.

> **Anything you would have done differently?**

Yes. As an entrepreneur there are a lot of things you would do different. Because with the entrepreneurial spirit you don't have initially, at least in my case, any exposure to running a practice, what does it mean – it's hands on experience. I am constantly looking at ways to improve and stay up on trends. I would have hired people sooner instead of wearing all the hats. I have hired on a part-time schedule based on their expertise.

> **How do you measure your success?**

My success is when people say, wow, I didn't realize that I could work with a financial planner. Ninety percent of my clients have never worked with a planner before. That means the world to me.

How did your preparation help you succeed?

I interviewed and interviewed and interviewed people and met people and asked questions and read and looked at about 75 business models. This is where I am going to start and I will adjust. What helped me prepare is being around people who have paved the way as fee-only planners.

What do you tell other people who ask for your advice?

Some people are cut out for being an entrepreneur and others are not. So don't be hard on yourself if you are not cut out for it. It is beyond a heavy lift. There are some days where you are questioning yourself over and over again whether you made the right choice. How you feel and what you have produced may not align up. It takes time to get ramped up and particularly if you are on the front end of the innovation curve. I was in that front end. My practice is pretty much virtual; I have people from across the country whom I have never met in person. That's a big trend change, leveraging technology. It will yield me great dividends. You have to be willing to pivot and have a great support system. Rethink, rethink what you are doing. Don't get so lost in the business that you are not thinking about moving the business forward.

Seek advice and counsel from others in your industry before you launch. I networked extensively with members of two organizations I joined: the Financial Planning Association and the National Association of Personal Financial Advisors, and later the Association of African American Financial Advisors. These are great places to meet thought leaders to give you practical and theoretical advice.

What books or resources did you use or recommend others to use?

I am more of a case study article reader. [Michael Gerber's] *The E-Myth* stands out for me.

What are some of the unexpected rewards and surprises?

Flexibility. Being able to put my own vision into play without the hindrance of people second-guessing or questioning you all the time because they are used to things a certain way. I love the freedom of entrepreneurship to make it up as you go along, as it feels right for you, because that is how the niche comes into play. A lot of people are, "Okay, do you serve women or do you serve Gen X?" I say no, I serve people who have not engaged with financial planning. Meeting people from diverse backgrounds and [who] believe in wealth for the common good.

Choosing my own clients. It's the freedom to be true to myself and attract clients who are like-minded, not necessarily the high-net-worth clients who other firms I had worked for service. I felt such a disconnect from the things that were important to them. It didn't resonate with me. I didn't see a lot of compassion or investment for the common good.

Lessons learned?

Hire talent early. I became a bottleneck as a solopreneur. As the momentum was building, I became overwhelmed. I didn't think about delegation. I had to dig myself out. I felt like I could do it all, and I had to do it all, if it was going to be done the right way.

That's not good. I learned in business school: you need to sacrifice income and hire a support team to free you up to focus on business generation activity. I didn't take heed to that. When you're in it, it's hard to step outside and put the theory into place.

And I have learned to carve out time for me. It's also important to make sure you are getting someone to help you.

Biggest challenge?

Waiting for society to embrace fee-only planners. And interestingly, flexibility. It wasn't starting the business that was challenging, but the refinement of it. It's a constant reinvention. I had to learn to be comfortable with making it up as I go along.

For example, I initially focused on offering comprehensive financial planning and investment management, but I now offer a smorgasbord of services, which includes hourly financial planning and consultations, and educational seminars. I must also work to stay extremely nimble, so I have time to accept outside opportunities, too. For instance, serving positions on the board of the Association of African American Financial Advisors.

How many employees do you have?

I have two part-time employees to help with administrative duties. I have used Upwork to hire administrative and marketing help.

WHERE TO FIND FINANCING TO GET STARTED

As you start and grow your business, you may find you need financing. The sooner you prepare, the easier it will be to get financing on favorable terms. Here are seven tips from Gerri Detweiler, education director for Nav (NAV.com), and coauthor of *Finance Your Own Business: Get on the Financing Fast Track*.

1. **Get a business bank account.** Separating business and personal accounts at the beginning will simplify bookkeeping, and many small-business financing sources will want to review business revenues.

2. **Start soon.** Soft-launch your business, if you're not ready to launch full-time. Why? Many lenders consider "time in business" when evaluating applications, and the longer your business has been around (even pre-revenue), the better. If you don't create a separate business entity, which is recommended, at least register a "DBA" (doing business as) with your state and obtain a business license if required.

3. **Build business credit.** Your business can have its own business credit reports and scores. Strong business credit opens up additional financing opportunities. A Nav survey found that business owners who understood their business credit were 41% more likely to get approved for financing. Get credit-building advice and monitor your business credit for free at Nav.com.

4. **Consider a small-business credit card.** Most small-business cards do not report to the owner's personal credit report unless you default, helping to protect your personal credit from the activity of your business. An added bonus: these cards can help build business credit. (For a list of issuer policies, visit Nav.com/report.) Keep in mind that small-business credit cards don't carry the same protections as consumer cards, so make sure you pay on time and don't incur debt you can't repay.

5. **Shop around.** There are dozens of financing options aimed at small businesses. Shop around so you can find the right financing at the best possible cost. A free e-guide called *Where's the Money? 10 Most Popular Financing Sources and How to Qualify* is available at SCORE.org.

6. **Scrutinize costs.** Unlike consumer financing, small-business financing offers don't have to include an Annual Percentage Rate (APR), and because there is no standard terminology, comparing costs can be confusing. Use free small-business loan calculators like those at Nav.com/business-loan-calculators to translate costs into an APR so you can compare offers.

7. **Protect your credit.** Business identity theft is a growing problem, too. It often goes undetected simply because small-business owners aren't reviewing their business credit, and don't realize there is a problem until unpaid debts pile up. Monitoring both personal and small-business credit on a regular basis can help you identify unusual activity, and hopefully stop it before it gets out of hand.

Black Women Entrepreneurs: The Good and Not-So-Good News

The number of African American women who are business owners has risen sharply, but why not revenues?

Dell Gines, the author of an intriguing new report from the Federal Reserve Bank of Kansas City, *Black Women Business StartUps*, loves this quote attributed to Reid Hoffman, cofounder of LinkedIn: "An entrepreneur is someone who will jump off a cliff and assemble an airplane on the way down." But for black women entrepreneurs, Gines quickly adds, "they do it with only a toothpick and a napkin." What he means is that black women entrepreneurs typically lack the resources and capital to launch, yet take off they do – in droves.

According to the *2018 State of Women-Owned Business* report commissioned by American Express, while the number of women-owned businesses grew an impressive 58% from 2007 to 2018, the number of firms owned by black women grew by a stunning 164%, nearly three times that rate. There were 2.4 million businesses owned by African American women in 2018, most owned by women 35 to 54. Black women are the only racial or ethnic group with more business ownership than their male peers, according to the Federal Reserve.

Black Women Entrepreneurs: The Revenue Lag

But not everything about black women entrepreneurs is so rosy.

American Express found that the gap is widening between the average revenue for businesses owned by women of color and those owned by nonminority women. For women of color, average revenue dropped from $84,000 in 2007 to $66,400 in 2018, while for nonminority businesses, revenue rose from $181,000 to $212,300. And the gap between African American women–owned businesses' average revenue and that of all women-owned businesses, Amex found, is the largest.

What's more, a catalyst for making the leap into entrepreneurship, the Federal Reserve Bank of Kansas City report said, "often was poor treatment and the perception of being undervalued in the workplace." The Amex report echoed this, noting that "higher unemployment rates, long-term unemployment and a much greater gender and racial pay gap have led women of color to start businesses at a higher rate out of necessity and the need to survive."

"It's pretty evident that one of the primary reasons for black women to start businesses is frustrations on the job," Gines told me. "They feel they can't get anywhere. We have been to seven cities doing the outreach and talked to a lot of black women. There's a feeling of being passed over for promotions, a sense of workplace fatigue, of being asked to train people to be their boss."

What's also evident, according to Gines: "The businesses tend to stay very small, and you don't see a lot of scalability."

On average, annual sales at businesses owned by black women are two times smaller than the next-lowest demographic group, Hispanic women, and close to five times smaller than for all women-owned businesses, according to the Federal Reserve. The average annual sales for businesses owned by black women was $27,752 in 2012 (the most recent figures available), compared to $143,731 for all women and $170,587 for white women.

Gines said those figures are unlikely to have shifted dramatically since 2012. "The gap persists at about the same level," he said.

Why So Many of the Businesses Are Micro

One reason so many of the businesses are micro is that many black women have difficulty accessing credit and face capital constraints, according to the Federal Reserve. That makes it hard to get the necessary funding to grow. And when black women try to borrow with lower income and lower wealth, "these factors make going for a loan that much more difficult," Gines said.

As a result, black women entrepreneurs tend to tap personal savings, and, all too frequently, retirement accounts, according to BC Clark, director of business development at the Nebraska Enterprise Fund, a nonprofit based in Omaha that works with many black women business owners.

"We definitely do not want them to do that because it took years to build and they might not get that money back," Clark told me. That's why the Nebraska Enterprise Fund puts on workshops to teach things like borrowing basics, how to write a business plan, creating a mission statement, and managing risk.

Starting a Side Business

For many black women business owners, the tiny size of their firms is intentional, regardless of the dearth of capital available from lenders. That's partly because they're often launched as side businesses out of financial necessity. Most black women entrepreneurs work part time in their businesses, less than 39 hours a week, according to the Federal Reserve report.

"Many black women founders may be single parents and need to have this dual income to support the household needs," said Gines.

Using a start-up as an initial second income stream can lead to positive results over the long haul. "It can mitigate the risk," Gines said. "Because the women are taking care of their families, they need to have a level of confidence before they can make that jump completely. Woman who are responsible for the household tend to keep the size of businesses artificially low because they're risk averse, need health insurance from a primary employer, and want to make sure everything is absolutely appropriate before taking the jump."

A Lack of Resources and Mentors

Another factor that slows growth: a lack of educational resources and mentors to help black women entrepreneurs ramp up their business knowledge.

While there are SCORE programs (retired business professionals offering free advice to start-up founders) in every major city, many black women cite a lack of mentors who understand their businesses and business models, or feel they can't connect culturally with the ones they meet, Gines said.

Two dominant entrepreneurial characteristics expressed by many black women business owners who participated in the 2017 focus groups conducted by the Federal Reserve of Kansas City were determination and self-learning. "Self-learning was a key characteristic that allowed many to start and grow a company in an environment with limited access to formal business knowledge and training," according to Gines.

Frequently, black women "don't know who to go to, where to go, and what organizations are out there that can support them," Gines said. This is one reason, he added, that "you see a lot of clustering in very few industries with a low barrier to entry – service businesses such as hair salons, catering, child day care centers and consulting."

The Optimistic Outlook

But Gines anticipates promising change coming.

"You are going to see a rise in black women doing business in professional services with the rapid increase in education levels for black women and their increased participation in the labor market, in fields such as accounting and engineering," he said.

Where to Get Advice

Both Gines and Clark advise black women entrepreneurs to look for know-how through a local chamber of commerce, the SBA's Women Business Centers, and women's business owner associations. Also, they say, take courses on entrepreneurship at a local community college.

It might make sense, too, to get certified as minority-owned and as a women's business on the federal, state, and city level, Clark said.

One parting thought: Faith and religious belief have also been important characteristics of many of the black women business owners who spoke with Gines. "They used their faith as both a source of motivation and a tool to support resiliency during difficult times," he said.

Amen to that.

Chapter Recap

In this chapter, you've met a woman of color facing a steep challenge in starting her own business in a field where there are few minority planners. She drew from her childhood passion about money and finances, and her inner drive to make a difference in people's lives, to launch her own advisory business in uncharted territory while relying on personal savings. And you have discovered ways to prepare to find start-up financing, as well as advice aimed at African American women seeking to start their own ventures.

YOUR TO-DO LIST

- Separate business and personal accounts to simplify bookkeeping.
- Start small as a side gig. A soft launch gives you time to work through the unexpected challenges.
- Continue journaling and writing your action lists each day.
- Look for advice through a local chamber of commerce, the SBA's Women Business Centers, and women's business owner associations.
- Take courses on entrepreneurship at a local community college.

C H A P T E R 3

Military to Merlot

Destiny Burns, CLE Urban Winery

Home is where the heart is and sometimes your newest love – a start-up. In April of 2015, Destiny Burns headed to the hometown of her childhood, Cleveland, Ohio, to create CLE Urban Winery, a handcraft winery and tasting room, in a 4,400-square-foot garage in Cleveland Heights.

It may seem like a bit of an unlikely next act for Burns, 54, who enjoyed a 20-year military career as a Navy Cryptologic Officer with posts around the world from Japan to the Persian Gulf. After she retired from active duty in 2003, she then spent 13 years in business development positions for defense contractors such as General Dynamics and Northrop Grumman. But she was restless.

A series of major life events shifted her mindset and gave her the impetus to step it up. First, she turned 50. Second, her marriage of 26 years came to an end. Her daughter, Aimee, had graduated from college and was on her own, and for the first time in more than 20 years, Burns, then living in Northern Virginia, was footloose. "I had always dreamed of having my own business. I had a desire to do something different and to, well, feed my soul," says Burns. "It wasn't easy walking away from the income I was making working for a defense contractor, but I was drained."

In time, she decided to return to Cleveland to spend her next chapter. "No matter where I lived around the world, Cleveland was my home," says Burns. "It represented family and a place where I had always found happiness. My mom (Donna), two sisters (Denys and Debbie), and one brother (Dennis) live here in Cleveland and it was always home for all of us.

"My favorite thing about Cleveland as a kid? Following the sports teams here. We never missed a Browns game after church at my grandmother's house, and I used to take my little brother to Indians games in the summer – sitting out in the cheap seats in the bleachers getting sunburned! When you're born and raised here, it's in your DNA to be a fan, no matter how bad the teams are."

Once the decision to go home again was made, Burns began her inner journey to explore that MRI of her soul: to identify the things that she had loved in her life, and the times that brought a smile and satisfaction, a sense of well-being. And her thoughts kept circling back to food and wine. "I have been a full-blown foodie for ages, and I loved tasting and studying about different food and wine as I trekked and was stationed from the Middle East to Italy to Hawaii. I began to hone in on the concept of creating a 'lifestyle' business that was centered on great food and wine," she says.

After roughly two years of groundwork, she launched her winery in July of 2016. Burns's business prototype was originally inspired by the Olney Winery, a storefront winery in Maryland that she patronized while living in the D.C. area. But her true inspiration came from the robust craft brewery community in Cleveland. "I wanted to create a craft brewery-style winery embedded in the heart of the city," says Burns. What happens is that the business takes the vineyard part and much of the risk associated with that process out of it. "I'm not a grower and I don't desire to be. My business, CLE Urban Winery, creates its own wine using grapes sourced from California, Washington, and other parts of the country."

Burns sells wine by the glass from 20 different varieties, for $8 to $12. Bottles start at $20 and go up to $40. Other offerings include a wine club, wine education classes, live music, tango lessons, and yoga classes. She also serves small food dishes, such as meat and cheese, dips, and spreads. The results have been promising.

So far, Burns's business has monthly net revenues exceeding $30,000 in the tasting room and $10,000 from sales to local restaurants, which is ample to service her debt and more, she says. All told, her first full year revenue topped $500,000 and she is on track for 20% year-over-year revenue growth in her second full year in business in 2018, and she turned a profit in 2018. She continues to expand sales to high-end grocery stores and continues to add restaurant accounts. "In 2019, we are introducing a curated selection of beer and spirits to the menu as well as planning to install a wine on tap system in the Tasting Room (to reduce costs as well as our carbon footprint), and to begin manufacturing wine ice cream," she says. She is also pondering the possibility of franchising her concept.

And she employed 18 workers (several part-time) by the end of 2018.

Burns, like other older entrepreneurs, has plenty of arrows in her quiver – a solid work ethic, management experience, a vibrant network of business contacts, and access to capital.

Launching in a Male-Dominated Field

Burns owes her success in part to being toughened up from years working in a male-dominated field. When I asked Burns about her challenges as a woman starting a business, she was quick to say there were challenges, but not because she was a woman.

"I have not really encountered any specific bias or issues related to my gender or age," she told me. "I have spent my entire adult and professional life in a man's world … first the U.S. military and then as an executive in the defense sector. Most entrepreneurs I encounter are also men. I am comfortable in male-dominated business situations. I just don't see myself as any different and that's how I conduct myself."

Her saving grace was her experience. She tapped the same skills to sell her business model to lenders that she'd used in her postmilitary career when making the case why the government should award her company the business.

As I wrote in my previous book, *What's Next? Finding Your Passion and Your Dream Job in Your Forties, Fifties, and Beyond,* while each new business owner takes their own path, there's a shared backbone for those who succeed. Many entrepreneurs at this stage of life are spurred into action after experiencing a life crisis, or major personal shift of some kind, perhaps a health issue, or a divorce as Burns did, or someone close to them dying at a young age. And each person has a flexible time horizon for their venture. Burns gave herself two years to plot a plan. She was also fortunate to have some outside investments, retirement savings, and a pension in place to ease the transition to her new line of work. Plus, she could keep working earning income as a contractor initially as she worked on her business plan. "I worked full-time as a defense contractor for a year from Cleveland as I built and started up my business. I quit my job two weeks before I opened the winery," she says.

You might know you want to do something new but don't have the nerve to do it yet. Take a breath. "You have to trust yourself," says Burns. "For me, it was really hard to leave a great job and the money behind, but once I decided that I could do this, that this is what I wanted to do, I drew the line in the sand and kept going forward. One key for me was to do at least one thing every day to move the concept forward until it becomes a reality."

Making It Work

I asked Destiny to look back and share her thoughts on her shift to starting her own winery and tasting room.

> **Kerry: What did starting your own business mean to you personally?**
>
> Destiny: Starting my own business was a dream come true and the start of a brand new life for me. I literally left everything behind – my home, my job, my friends, my volunteer activities – to move back to my hometown and start all over again on my own terms. I totally made the right decision!

Were you confident that you were doing the right thing? Any second-guessing?

It was a big leap of faith, but I felt much more confident making that leap after doing extensive research, planning, and forecasting as part of my business plan. Even so – it was still a major risk, even if it was a calculated one. Once I signed the lease on the winery space, however … that was the point of no return where I was determined to make it successful no matter what!

Anything you would have done differently?

Nothing! I have enjoyed every day and every step of this journey. Even when it was two steps forward and one step back. I love creating something, making a difference, and bringing something cool and wonderful to my life and to my hometown.

How do you measure your success?

I did not go into this to be a millionaire (although that would be awesome!) … I measure my success in traditional ways like being able to pay all my bills, by being the best boss I can be for my staff, by receiving good customer reviews, and by there being more black ink on my business financials than red ink. I equally measure my success by working with and donating to local charitable organizations, by learning something every day, by seeking opportunities to partner with other local small businesses, by supporting local musicians and artists, and by helping and by mentoring others as part of my entrepreneurial journey.

How big a role did financial rewards play in your decision?

I was making a ton of money in the corporate world. Money was not a primary motivator in becoming an entrepreneur. To me, the qualitative rewards are more important.

How did your preparation help you succeed?

My preparation was absolutely critical to my success, especially in such a high-failure-rate industry. Finding a true niche in the market and executing with consistency, passion, and integrity according to plan was key to my success.

What do you tell other people who ask for your advice?

Do your homework. A great idea without a market or a customer is just an idea and nothing more. Educate yourself, especially about business financials and processes. Build your dream team: staff, consultants, vendors, mentors – you can't do it alone. Find your tribe.

What books or resources did you use or recommend others to use?

I have implemented the Entrepreneurial Operating System (EOS) in my business based on the book *Traction: Get a Grip on Your Business* by Gino Wickman and it has transformed our business operations and strategy. I also highly recommend *Scaling Up: How a Few Companies Make It … And Why the Rest Don't* by Verne Harnish, *Scale: Seven Proven Principles to Grow Your Business and Get Your Life Back* by Jeff Hoffman and David Finkel, *The Pumpkin Plan* by Mike Michalowicz, and *Start with Why: How Great Leaders Inspire Everyone to Take Action* by Simon Sinek.

What are some of the unexpected rewards and surprises?

The biggest surprise is the responsibility I feel to the winery brand I have created. It is bigger than me. I feel like it has a life and destiny of its own and it's my job now to shepherd it, advocate for it, and take it to the state it is meant to become.

Lessons learned?

You can't work ON your business if you are working IN your business. An owner-dependent business can only grow as far as the owner's stamina and sanity can take it.

You have to groom and grow others in your company to perform the operations of the business so that you as the owner/visionary can be developing and implementing growth strategies rather than just bringing in the bacon.

Biggest challenge?

Cash flow. Cash is king when it comes to operating and growing a business successfully.

Kerry's Blueprint for Entrepreneurs

Get Financially Fit

It can take a few years or more to get a business rocking, even one that doesn't have bricks and mortar that you're piloting out of your home. Craft a budget to see where you can trim back expenses. Pay down any credit cards where you're carrying a balance. Debt is a dream killer. When you're financially fit, you're nimble. You have choices. You have the financial security that can fund your start-up through personal savings. And when you're starting your own business, you may not be able to pay yourself initially, so this ballast can help you ride out those initial months.

You might consider downsizing your home, which might result in not having a mortgage to pay, or you may opt to move to a town where the cost of living is more affordable, as Burns did.

Consider Working for Someone Else While You Get the Wheels in Motion

Burns did. She was able to work remotely for her employer pulling in the same salary for an entire year from her new Cleveland abode. "It was fantastic to earn my D.C. income in a Cleveland economy," she told me. And that was a huge advantage when it came to stashing away funds for her new business-to-be. "I also retooled my lifestyle to save as much money as possible, so I could have that little cushion and afford to take that jump off the cliff," says Burns. "I did not do this willy-nilly."

Continue to Save for Retirement

When you no longer have access to an employer-sponsored retirement plan such as a 401(k), it can be far too easy to skip or skimp on setting funds aside. Do your homework on your options for retirement plan savings, from a SEP-IRA to a solo 401(k). You can ask your tax accountant or financial planner for help deciding what's best for you. The IRS.gov website can provide the nitty-gritty.

Burns, for example, merged her previous employer retirement plans into a SEP-IRA, and is contributing to it annually, with plans to do so until she is 70½, when the tax benefit disappears. She also has a pension from her years of military service.

According to a BMO Wealth Management survey of 400 small-business owners, only a fraction of America's entrepreneurs are prepared for retirement. A striking 75% of survey respondents age 18 to 64 have saved less than $100,000 for retirement. Those age 45 to 64 are only marginally more prepared: 32% have over $100,000 in retirement accounts and only 11% have more than $500,000. I was pleased, however, to see that 39% of business owners age 45 to 64 – the ones closing in on retirement – had traditional IRAs or Roth IRAs, and 29% were saving in 401(k)-type accounts.

Why don't more small-business owners save for retirement? "The business is their retirement plan," says David Deeds, the Schulze Professor of Entrepreneurship at the University of St. Thomas in Minneapolis. "The plan is that when they retire, they are either going to transfer the business to a family member in exchange for a share of future wealth or a buyout or they are going to sell it off and turn that into cash. There is a risk level to it," adds Deeds, who is also editor-in-chief of EIX, the Entrepreneur & Innovation Exchange (EIX.org), a social media learning platform designed to improve the success rate of new business ventures. "If the business fails, your wealth goes away.

For small-business owners, it's not that they don't want to save for retirement outside of their businesses. Their priority is to plow earnings back into the business to keep it growing, so they rarely pay themselves a big salary. "If you are a small-business owner, much of your wealth is trapped in your business.

Ways to Set Up Saving for Retirement

"The problem is in order to diversify that wealth, you have to remove that wealth from the business, and, in essence, remove some of the lifeblood from the business," Deeds says. "Taking money out impinges on growth prospects and it can make it hard to maintain the business."

The four main options: a SEP-IRA, a SIMPLE IRA, a Solo 401(k), and a SIMPLE 401(k). For all but SEP-IRAs, a business can be a sole proprietorship, a partnership, a limited liability company, or a corporation.

A SEP-IRA is a tax-deferred retirement plan like a traditional IRA and is great if you're the company's only employee (as I am). In 2019, you can contribute up to $56,000. The account is tax-free until you withdraw the money at retirement. Usually there is a penalty for removing the funds before age 59½, and you must start withdrawing the money at age 70½. One caveat: If you have employees, you generally must also fund SEP-IRAs for them.

A SIMPLE IRA is a retirement plan for business owners with 100 or fewer employees. Contributions are pre-tax and taken directly out of employee paychecks, similar to a 401(k). In 2019, your contribution couldn't exceed $13,000, or $16,000 if you're 50 or older.

A Solo 401(k) is for self-employed people without employees (except perhaps a spouse). The IRS let you contribute, pre-tax, a $56,000 maximum in 2019, or up to $6,000 more if you're 50 or older.

A SIMPLE 401(k) is for businesses with 100 or fewer employees. You and your employees can borrow against the money in your 401(k) accounts and make penalty-free withdrawals due to financial hardship. Maximum contribution in 2019: $13,000. The catch-up limit is still $3,000.

Do the Paperwork

Most small businesses require permits and licenses from your town, county, and state. These differ by location, and normally need to be renewed annually. It's also shrewd to touch base with your town officials and local business owners to get a grip on the existing local regulations.

Shop for Health Insurance

If you are under 65, you will need to buy your own health insurance, since you won't be covered by an employer plan and will be too young for Medicare. Compare premiums, deductibles, and out-of-pocket costs from multiple insurers. Research the plans and prices on HealthCare.gov, or the site for your state health care exchange, if your state offers one.

A health insurance broker can help. You might be able to find one at the National Association of Health Underwriters (NAHU. org). Check to see whether your preferred doctors are in-network. Also consider opening a tax-advantaged Health Savings Account (HSA). This account works in combination with a high-deductible health insurance plan, which can help keep your health insurance costs down, and you can use the HSA to save money for future health care expenses.

Redeploy Your Existing Skills

"When I was working for the defense contractor I was focused on business development, and writing proposals for contracts worth hundreds of millions of dollars," says Burns. "I had to make the case for why the government should give my employer the business, so I had those communication skills."

As she was putting together her business plan and looking for lenders to work with, she applied those same communication and analytical skills to sell her concept. "It's all about the value proposition for them, what would make my business successful, and analyzing what was already here in Cleveland in terms of wine bars and wine-related businesses."

Do Your Prep Work

Once Burns landed on the type of business she was attracted to starting, she reached out to the owners of the winery in Maryland that triggered her interest in opening one, and hired the owner as a consultant. And since she was clueless about how to make wine, she tracked down a winemaker she contacted via the director of the winemaking program at Kent State's Ashtabula campus. Her connection there introduced her to Dave Mazzone, a knowledgeable wine professional who has worked in Napa Valley, and is also a Cleveland native.

Burns and Mazzone then spent a week working with the team in Maryland to get a bead on how they operated and a rundown of how they got started and have managed to sustain profitability.

Add the Skills Necessary

Burns, for instance, earned a certification in food service. Community colleges, business schools, and other postsecondary institutions offer classes on the basics of starting a business, and there are also online tutorials. For instance, you might want to sharpen your marketing or finance chops, or get an understanding of employment law.

Do One Thing Daily to Work Toward Your Goal

"During the nearly two years before I launched, I made it a point to keep at it every day, even when I was still working and traveling for my full-time job," says Burns. "Sometimes all that meant was making a phone call for some market research, but it helped me crystallize what I was doing. It kept it real."

Line Up Sources of Funding

If you're in decent financial shape with no debt – or at least very little beyond a mortgage – you will likely have several options for funding your start-up. A good place to start is Govloans.gov, the federal government's site for entrepreneurs seeking grants and financing, and usa.gov/funding-options, a guide to a variety of ways to finance your business, including loans backed by the government and funding programs. Other sources of funding could include personal savings, friends and family, banks and credit unions, and crowdfunding websites such as Kickstarter.

Assemble Your Team

You can't do it alone. "I own my dream and now own my business. But I also have an accountant, I have lawyers, and I use the services of a payroll company," says Burns. "I need all that support."

For now, she has several full-time employees, including winemaker Mazzone and hourly workers for the tasting room. "I was nervous about hiring people," says Burns. "As an officer in the military, I know about leading and managing people, and how tough it can be."

Entrepreneurs who succeed are generally the ones who have asked for help. You'll definitely need a list of professionals to support you, from a lawyer to a tax accountant. And like other second acts, it's always good to try out the job first as an apprentice or moonlight to be sure it's right for you. A great place to start your research is at AARP's Small Business website (aarp.org/work/small-business). You'll find helpful resources from building a business plan to funding advice and more.

AARP and the SBA have formed a multipronged collaboration to promote entrepreneurship. The partnership hosts Encore Mentoring events that offer counseling, training, and mentoring on small-business creation. Through online educational resources and in-person events, budding entrepreneurs get help on assessing whether they're ready to start a business.

You can begin by contacting your town or county's Small Business Development Center.

Seek Out Virtual Advice

Virtual adviser Alice (helloalice.com) is a platform that uses artificial intelligence to let female entrepreneurs connect with other business owners, government resources, potential funders, and mentors. Alice provides assistance from some of the top entrepreneurship sources in the country, including the Case Foundation, the Kauffman Foundation, and the SBA. Her promise: to "connect founders with the resources they need to scale."

By asking Alice, women looking to build businesses should be able to find answers to questions about financing, strategy, marketing, and legal needs. For starters, it's free (for now) and it's not technically restricted to women, although Alice is coded with women in mind. You enter your profile based on your industry, start-up stage, revenue, and location. Alice then curates your needs based on what you're looking for – say, a tech solution or an attorney – and the answers are different for every user. The goal is to connect entrepreneurs with resources they can't find in their location or that aren't on their radar.

Take Inventory

The checklist for launching a company from the SBA (sba.gov) is a great place to begin. It helps you review your situation, identify a niche, analyze the market, and get a sense of your financial picture.

Write a Business Plan

There's no strict model to follow, but in general, a simple plan – which you'll have to submit to get a loan or other financing – should be about 20 pages. I recommend seeking out a SCORE counselor to help you fine-tune, if possible. Essentially, here's what you'll need:

- ☐ An executive summary that explains what your company will do, who the customers will be, why you are qualified to run it, how you'll sell your goods and services, and your financial outlook.
- ☐ A detailed description of the business, its location, your management team, and your staffing requirements. You'll also need to include information about your industry and competition.
- ☐ A market analysis that targets your customers more specifically, including age, gender, and geographic location. The analysis also will describe your sales and promotional strategy to reach them.
- ☐ A realistic forecast of start-up outlays – cost of raw materials, equipment, employee salaries, marketing materials, insurance, utilities, and fees for attorneys and accountants – and how much you expect to sell and to earn.

Your eventual success in running a small business will come from having a strong vision of what it is you want from the very start. How much time can you really give to it? How flexible do you want it to be? Is it too late to really make a go of it?

Brace for Holdups

Finally, you should expect that it will take at least three years before your business gets on its feet financially, but be prepared for it to take longer. "Don't give up," says Burns. "I wasn't deterred when my loan was rejected the first time. I picked myself up and went back to the mentors at the small-business development center and tweaked my proposal, then went back to another bank. I had two other banks lined up if that one didn't work. I was determined to get the funding I needed."

The biggest reward: "I pinch myself to be able to work in this space that I built, bringing business to this neighborhood and being part of a community, and, of course, kicking back and sipping on a glass of my own full-bodied, piquant Syrah."

GETTING YOUR NAME IN LIGHTS

How good are you at selling yourself? Whether you have a stand-alone business, or are a consultant, work-at-home crafter, or self-employed plumber or carpenter, to build a successful second act as an entrepreneur, you have got to know how to do the old soft shoe.

Here are nine strategies to help you promote yourself and your business to catch the eye of new clients and projects.

1. **Work the websites.** Upwork can lead you to online positions; Freelancer.com to project-based work; and VirtualVocations.com to telecommuting jobs ranging from grant writing to graphic design to bookkeeping. On TaskRabbit, you can sign up for jobs ranging from fix-it person to personal assistant. LinkedIn ProFinder is another matchmaking service.

   Setting up an account is free on these sites, but you usually pay a percentage of your earnings. Upwork, for example, charges fees of 20%, 10%, or 5% depending on the total amount you've billed with the client.

2. **Leverage social media.** In addition to having a LinkedIn page, you might want Facebook, Instagram, Pinterest, and Twitter pages for your business. Ask your peers to see which networks they use professionally. Photographers often showcase their work on Instagram. Pinterest is popular if you're in the retail or consumer goods business.

   Whether you're a skilled artisan, tradesperson, or hair stylist, your work might easily lend itself to visual showcasing to people you are friends with, or who follow you, via an online professional portfolio of photos on Facebook, Instagram, Pinterest and, yes, LinkedIn.
   You can build your brand and reputation online and market your services by posting images of completed projects. Encourage satisfied customers to tout your talents. Consider recording and posting a YouTube video of a work project from start to finish featuring your specialized skills and process. Wear your pride in your workmanship and show it off.

3. **Mine your network.** Let people know you're looking for clients. Be bold. Announce your services from time to time on Facebook or post word of a job you've just completed. Join industry groups on LinkedIn.

   Face-to-face networking, such as joining trade associations affiliated with your line of work and perhaps a labor union, is a must, whether you're a landscaper, house painter, plumber, or tiler. Talking to people in your community is fundamental to adding new clients. Word of mouth is what will bring you new work. That means also reaching out to people who belong to your religious organization, connecting with other parents at your kid's (or grandkid's) sporting events, doing volunteer work, and getting involved with your local chamber of commerce.

4. **Keep building your network.** When you're engaged in a project or assignment, collect names and contact information for all the people you work with. One project or temporary assignment often leads to others.

5. **Be active in industry groups.** If there's a certain industry you're interested in, join a local association or organization connected with it. Attend industry and professional meetings and conferences. Monitor the association job boards and let other members know you're open for business.

6. **Reach out to nonprofits, too.** They often hire project-based or contract professionals. You might even offer your services pro bono to get your name out there and gain references for future jobs.

7. **Know what you're worth.** Research the going rate for what you do. Many self-employed workers have websites where they post their rates. Or contact some of them in your field and ask. If they're reluctant to share, they might open up if you explain you're looking into entering the field and you don't want to undercut others on price.

8. **Launch your own website.** If you plan to make self-employment work your full-time occupation, you'll want to build a strong brand. It will help you build your clientele by establishing you as an expert in your field and someone who can be trusted.

The cornerstone in online branding efforts will be a website, blog, or combination of the two. You can post articles to demonstrate your insight into the industry, share a full portfolio of your work, and include testimonials from past clients and supervisors. Low-cost options such as WordPress, GoDaddy, Wix, or Squarespace, where monthly fees start around $10 per month, make it easy to customize your own site by adding photos and text to templates.

You can launch a single-page website with a professional photo, detailing your professional background and interests – kind of like a spotlighted resume – and build on it later. If you need something more complex, you can always hire a professional, but expect to pay much more.

After you have the basics set up, it's a good idea to post new content regularly. Regular blog posts will boost your site's ranking with search engines, making it more likely that prospective clients will view your page.

(Continued)

GETTING YOUR NAME IN LIGHTS (*Cont'd*)

9. **Don't be shy.** Some people are naturals at selling themselves face to face. If you're not, consider taking a public-speaking class at a community college. Most courses cover techniques for such things as managing communication anxiety, speaking clearly, and tuning in to your body language. Sign up for an acting or improvisational comedy workshop; these can help you build your confidence and stage presence. Or join Toastmasters. Groups of about 20 people meet weekly for an hour or two. You learn how to focus your attention away from your own anxieties and concentrate on your message and audience. Finally, consider working with a personal career coach.

PRACTICE HOVERING

My acronym, HOVER, introduced in my book *Love Your Job*, stands for Hope, Optimism, Value, Enthusiasm, Resilience. It symbolizes looking down, surveying the situation, and then strategically tapping these five basic ingredients to create the change you need in your job and your life.

Hope is vital. Believe that you can reach your goals, and you will find a way to do so. My goal is for you to work on developing that crucial internal psychological muscle as you read along through this book.

Optimism involves taking an upbeat view of your work and your potential for success. For me, this is a core factor in loving what you do every day. When you're optimistic, you have a sense of enthusiasm that you can tap to take action – to see possibilities and solutions to problems at work.

This ability to have a can-do approach lets you bounce back quicker from rejection and not feel the urge to throw in the towel. It also opens your eyes to see how "you can" bring about change, not focus on how "you can't."

In my opinion, optimistic people tend to succeed in work and life because they're willing to take risks. They aren't afraid to fail because they know they will find a way to make it work and are willing to be patient and wait for it all to play out. They chip away at whatever the issue may be with the confidence that in the end, things will improve. And with each little chip, things will improve.

One way to develop optimism is to focus on what's going right and stop thinking so much about what is going wrong – or could. Again, I find that writing a journal can help with this. If you notice that the same concerns, worries, and pessimistic views keep cropping up, it will help you see that you need to either make some changes, or let it go. And always keep a "good" list, or a gratitude list, as some people call it. Use your list to reset your day, every day. Be grateful.

Optimism streams from gratitude. Thankfulness is a great remedy to what ails you. Routinely take note of the things you like the most about your business. Give yourself a moment or two to be grateful for whatever those things are. Reach out and thank someone who does a good turn for you or made your work shine in some way. It makes you both feel good. An email is fine, but a handwritten note is always classy.

I try to think of at least one work-related thing I am grateful for each day. And so it goes. Interactions with others, even virtual ones, can get you unstuck and make you feel that someone notices you and your work. You feel valued.

There are days when I'm dazed with deadlines, and I'm uneasy with the pressure. But when I pause and remember these good moments, those negative feelings dissipate. It's a dose of mental relief and an opportunity to push the restart button. Try it.

Value is critical. This means having the inner confidence to know that if you put out the effort, you will get results or see progress. It means you yourself value your own work, skills, and talents. It means you believe in yourself. That inner compass, pulled by confidence, will help direct your actions. It's subtle, but those around you will sense and respond to it.

One way to build your sense of value is to continually be learning new things. To deal effectively with the challenges of starting a new business, it helps to be engaged in changing yourself. The most creative people I know frequently get involved in learning or self-improvement efforts. It's fun. When you do so, everything else around you becomes more stimulating. When you're gaining knowledge, you see the world around you. You spot things. You listen better. Your mind turns on.

So if you can just do one thing to make a change right now, learn something new. If you can't make it work related, do it in the context of your life. Sign up for a series of lectures at your local community center or library. Something as simple as participating in a monthly book club can get your mind engaged.

When we feel valued both from inside ourselves and from others, we give back to others and perhaps ultimately to our clients. Everyone gains.

Enthusiasm is the elusive get-up-and-go factor that boosts your energy and helps you tackle changes both internal and external. When you're enthusiastic, people want what you have. They want to be around you. They want you to be on their team. Enthusiasm is infectious, and it's invigorating.

The bottom line: Being eager to try new things and see the upside of a project can lead you to interesting assignments and opportunities that will bring happiness to your work life in ways you may never have envisioned.

(*Continued*)

PRACTICE HOVERING (*Cont'd*)

Resilience, or a knack for springing back in the face of adversity or failure, is imperative in achieving happiness at work. Resilient people resist the urge to get bogged down in the past, and instead keep looking toward the future. They're curious. They keep learning.

You can teach yourself to be resilient. You can learn to be more comfortable in an environment where nothing stays the same and the old ways may no longer work. That's the heart of running your own shop, to be honest. When you gain resilience, you can create a more successful career path while finding greater enjoyment in the rest of your life.

So get your HOVER on. Not everyone can put all these pieces together at the same time, of course, but it's what you're striving toward.

Chapter Recap

In this chapter, we've learned how a successful entrepreneur tapped into her passion and skills to help outline and motivate her quest to start a new business. And we've been reminded of the importance of reining in personal debt and continuing to save for retirement. Finally, we've opened our eyes to the reality that nothing happens overnight when it comes to getting your business into the black. Expect it to take three years to start to gain traction.

YOUR TO-DO LIST

- Consider where you might want to live and launch. Is it a good idea to move to someplace where the living expenses are cheaper or you have a built-in network of early customers and supporters?
- Map out ways you can keep earning an income while you pull together your business plan.
- Do a budget and see where you can trim costs, and pay down debt to get nimble.
- Keep saving for retirement.
- Be grateful and say thanks.

4

Cockpit to the Coffee Shop

Mike Foster, FosterHobbs Coffee Roasters

Decades of downing cups of crummy airplane coffee, mixed with milk to make it drinkable, were the driving force for former airline pilot Mike Foster's venture, FosterHobbs Coffee Roasters, an artisan supplier of specialty-grade Arabica coffee beans, in High Point, North Carolina. You can't get many beverages there: iced coffee, yes; espresso, no. The attention is on ground or whole beans that coffee devotees can brew at home or at the office.

"I discovered my passion for coffee on my first transatlantic flight in the mid-1990s as a pilot for American Airlines," says Foster, 59. "The coffee I drank trying to keep my eyes open was awful. I made it a hobby to seek out new coffee shops wherever I had layovers."

In 2009, after 23 years with the airline, Foster accepted an early retirement from his six-figure salary and captain's perch at American Airlines, with a dream of creating his own coffee shop.

Like a pilot crossing items off a preflight review, he set about this with focused planning. Foster spent two years meticulously doing research and bouncing his ideas off a coffee industry specialist. The consultant counseled him to skip serving specialty beverages, and instead build a possibly more lucrative business retailing freshly roasted high-end coffee beans.

To confirm that was the right recommendation, he posed the question to a past president of a large grocery store chain, the head of a prepackaged food company, a district manager of a specialty grocery store chain, a Starbucks trainer, one of Microsoft's former marketing gurus, a coffee-brewing-equipment expert, and a master roaster. They all agreed with the industry specialist: stick to marketing beans.

So in 2011, Foster began the drawn-out route of beginning the business. He called it FosterHobbs, linking his surname and his wife Pam's maiden name. A designer shaped a logo set on a winged coffee bean, which evokes his flying days. With a bricks-and-mortar store in High Point, a city of around 110,000 residents near Winston-Salem and Greensboro, he knew he'd need to have a significant online sales presence to support the business, so he set up an e-commerce website.

In 2012, Foster signed a rental agreement on a retail space. He devoted the next six months to getting the property ready to roast green coffee beans and peddle them in pound-size bags over the counter to customers. Start-up money was tapped to pay for the equipment and initial stock of supplies ($10,000), plus about $6,000 to design the website. That capital came from personal savings and small loans from three silent backers, who each got a 5% share of the business. Over the next three years, the business also pulled an additional $50,000 from a credit union line of credit.

The roastery and retail store finally opened in December of 2012. Like most start-ups, it was a quiet launch. "We made $800 the first week. At that point, I was just excited someone bought our beans," says Foster.

Today, his clientele can buy bags of 100% Arabica whole bean or ground specialty-grade coffee from Brazil, Colombia, Costa Rica, Ethiopia, Peru, and Sumatra. The company roasts small amounts of beans at a time so it can offer the freshest coffee. The store's best sellers: Costa Rica, LaMinita, Sumatran, and their own creation: Red-Head Blend.

By September of 2015, FosterHobbs broke into the black on its 1,000th day of operation. For 2018, it brought in revenues of close to $100,000. Sales are picking up at an average rate of 20% a month over the same month last year, as new customers have bought Foster's freshly roasted coffee beans at around $13 or $14 for a 12-ounce bag. And Foster has an increasing number of wholesale accounts, including local coffee shops and restaurants, and one major retailer, The Fresh Market, an upscale grocer in Winston-Salem.

The biggest problem has been the shop's lifeless web presence. The plan had been to sell 80% of its beans online. The site wasn't user-friendly, Foster told me. "My own lack of tech savvy held us back."

So he and his spouse overhauled the website and concocted a new social media marketing approach. Pam is now engaged in ramping up FosterHobbs' Facebook, Instagram, Pinterest, and Twitter accounts, and online sales are finally on the rise. The business is now almost debt free, and Foster and his wife plan to use positive cash flow beginning in 2019 to continue to pump up e-commerce/marketing.

For now, Foster and his wife are the only employees. "Assuming e-commerce grows as expected, I am sure we will end up hiring employees," he says. After all, his vision for FosterHobbs is to ultimately become a major player in the Southeast, and perhaps nationwide. Flight attendants – prepare for takeoff.

Making It Work

I asked Mike to look back and share his thoughts on his shift to starting his own coffee company.

Kerry: What did starting your own business mean to you personally?

Mike: Freedom to determine my own future.

Were you confident that you were doing the right thing? Any second-guessing?

I was confident.

Anything you would have done differently?

Started earlier in my life and saved more start-up funds.

How do you measure your success?

Enjoying your work and knowing your purpose in life.

How big a role did financial rewards play in your decision?

Knowing the potential rewards for both my family and how it could benefit the ministry arm of our coffee company, Fill the Gap Concerts, our effort to expose more people to the Christian faith through music, is encouraging.

How did your preparation help you succeed?

Doing community work while younger gave me confidence taking on managed risk, and I studied coffee for about 10 years before I left the airline industry.

What do you tell other people who ask for your advice?

Aim high, dream big, while researching like crazy.

What books or resources did you use or recommend others to use?

How to Win Friends and Influence People by Dale Carnegie; *A Blessed Life* by Pastor Robert Morris.

What are some of the unexpected rewards and surprises?

Learned my purpose in life.

Lessons learned?

Put more effort into online earlier in the process.

Biggest challenge?

I was developing a nonprofit public charity 501(c)(3), Fill the Gap Concerts, at the exact same time I was developing FosterHobbs Coffee roasters. Both required a lot of my time.

Fear of Success, Not Failure

When it comes to opening your own business and handling the day-to-day management, from stressing over finding clients and work to managing cash flow, there's lots to make you feel anxious. Trust me. You might even call it borderline fear, which in essence can be a good thing because it shoots you through with a jolt of adrenaline. But there's also the downside: it can be paralyzing. There's never the *right* time to make your move, to take the leap. You get stuck in the dream. It's safe to imagine what might be. It's a whole other ballgame when you verbalize, tell others, and start taking the actions to make it a reality. Something shifts. It's uncomfortable. The "what if" becomes "what now?"

Are you ready? Is your ego prepared to be the beginner, the newcomer, the one who has to ask for help and advice? Are you prepared to not always be the best, the winner, to make mistakes?

It's okay to be nervous. But it's not okay to let those doubts stop you from following a new path that might make your life a heck of a lot better in countless ways – personally and financially. One refrain I hear time and time again from successful entrepreneurs and those who have embarked on the self-employed path: "I never second-guessed my decision. I only wish I had done it sooner."

There's an inner assurance these successful mid-life entrepreneurs have that keeps them going, even when things get rocky.

The fact is, starting a new business is risky, and how you navigate that uncertainty will be unique to you. It's not a one-size-fits-all challenge. This quote from Rosa Parks resonates with me: "I have learned over the years that when one's mind is made up, this diminishes fear; knowing what must be done does away with fear."

To get some advice on what you can do to address your fears, I sat down with business and work coach Patricia DiVecchio, author of *Evolutionary Work: Unleashing Your Potential in Extraordinary Times* and president of International Purpose (internationalpurpose.com), based in Arlington, Virginia, who has been helping people for over three decades years manage fear and uncover their work potential and purpose.

Here's what she told me about conquering fear: "First, fear of success is greater than our fear of failure," she says. "I know how fear can stop me. Fear, or false evidence appearing real, is usually only in my head, but that doesn't stop it from speaking so loudly that I believe it's fact. It usually isn't. There is a saying that goes, 'Only believe half of what you think,' and I would recommend even less than that."

So, what prevents us from getting our greater work out in the world? What prevents us from moving forward? It's often the following, says DiVecchio:

1. Fear of losing something we see as having great value – which is sometimes just the comfort of the status quo and our pride.
2. Fear of not getting what we want or what we think is the best for ourselves. Here we find ourselves fearing success and failure – I believe it's more the fear of success. Could we handle it once we got it? Would we, if it's too much responsibility? Everyone will then have expectations of me.
3. Fear of being found out. The old imposter syndrome: maybe we just aren't who we say we are. In fact, we are usually more than we even think, and we are playing too small.

To get a grip on this, DiVecchio suggests thinking about these three concepts: See fear as an ally. Don't fear what you want most. Embrace your resistance.

Seriously? Fear as my ally, my pal? "Yes, fear can be your friend," she says. "It can be a great motivator, a great teacher. We don't see it like that. We tend to run away from fear, back or shy away from it, instead of stepping into it. You need to recognize it as something you can learn from. You need to shake hands with your fear and enlist it as a friend – a force to encourage forward movement, rather than something to hide from."

It always amazes me, though, that the people I have met who are wrestling with their inner dream of doing their own thing, do a lot of talk and no action. They complain about their current work or how bored they are on the job or burned out, but they are stuck.

"I agree," DiVecchio says. "It should be exciting to do something you've always wanted to do or are passionate about, but most people have a genuine fear of change, even if it is positive change. It's the unknown. We are afraid of the conflict that it might create, within and outside of ourselves, when we stand up for our true wants and needs. There's the fear of greater responsibility. Or if you are starting over in a new field, there's the fear of a downgrade in status, at least initially. That can come with a fear of a loss of power, respect, acceptance, and money. Funny, those same things can be scary in the reverse too – people are sometimes afraid of the gain of power, respect, acceptance, and money."

I had to shake my head. Who is fearful of success? "Getting what we want most in life can be scary," she says. "There's a huge accountability. It's work to *stay* successful. Plus, our sense of well-being is naturally based on the past and how things have always been. So if we are looking at moving into a business mid-life it's difficult to comprehend, again, the unknown. And it sounds funny, but we also fear success because we fear it's going to be more work, and we don't want to work that hard. One way to get a handle on this is to write down what emotions you feel when you start to visualize your new work life. What surfaces?"

Here are DiVecchio's six ways to help embrace fear and learn. Here are excerpts from our conversation.

1. **Draw your fear**. One client saw himself in a rickety old car, the only one on a pothole-filled road heading up a huge mountain. When you give a form or image to your fear, it makes it more concrete. Otherwise, fear is very nebulous and has us by our neck. This always works. I've had clients draw themselves encased in iron unable to move, in a castle with crocodiles in the moat and no drawbridge, with talking heads that say, "You don't know what you are doing."

2. **Write about it in a journal.** For my client in that car, when he wrote about the image, he determined it meant he could see there was no end in sight. He felt hopeless. Fear has something to teach you. It's telling you something. When you try to understand your drawing, it brings it to the top. Is the broken-down car out in the wilderness all about being scared to ask for help? It can be that clear.

3. **Draw what it would look like without the fear**. This alters your mindset. Maybe the road is even for my client. The sun is out. The sky is blue. When you picture the fear and act on it, you can overcome it.

4. **Do small acts**. Do one thing every day that you're fearful of doing. Keep track of them in your journal. This exercise starts to build up your "risk" muscle. For example, you might make a phone call that you have been putting off. Before you call, compose what want to say, your objectives for the call, and imagine the person on the other end as being as human as you are. People are always willing to talk about themselves and their work. Engage them. Make the conversation valuable for them.

5. **Write about what comes to you easily and effortlessly that is exciting (the three E's).** If you can identify your innate skills and talents, you can package that and create work from it. You're going to be the most successful, the happiest, and probably better

rewarded financially because you are doing work based on your strong skills and talents. Our innate skills are our strongest – more than what we gain from education and experience.

6. **Interview four or five people in your life – friends, family or colleagues – and ask them what they think you are good at.** Sometimes we are the last to get our true worth. Look at the patterns that emerge from their answers. Look at what's repeating itself. If everyone says you have wonderful communication skills, pay attention to that.

"We've all invested a lot of time and effort in crafting our lives, so we are hardly going to let go of the status quo or even change it for the better without a lot of kicking and screaming. But there is something inside of you that is calling you to change, to face the fear, and take forward action," notes DiVecchio.

Moreover, she adds – and I wholeheartedly can attest – once you start acting, fear does dissipate.

Chapter Recap

In this chapter, you learned that having a dream for a business is just the starting point. You need to be willing and able to shift that vision as you move forward. You'll need to expend effort on diligent research, which can easily take two years to reveal a viable plan. But you don't have to go it alone. Working with an industry consultant can prevent you from trying to reinvent the wheel. Finally, be realistic. Few startups are overnight smashes. Creating a strong business is a process.

YOUR TO-DO LIST

- Track down an industry consultant who can provide some clear-eyed perspective. Ask for recommendations from other small-business owners in your industry.
- Focus on what it is you want to sell or a service you want to provide. Be specific. You might work through this mental process of elimination in your journal to discover the essence of what you want your business to represent. It's easy to think too broadly, or try to bite off too much, at least initially. Keep it simple.
- Write down what emotions you feel when you start to visualize your new work life as an entrepreneur. What surfaces?
- Is there fear? If so, take time to do some of the exercises outlined in this chapter: drawing the fear, journaling about what you see as your core skills, and asking others for input.

CHAPTER 5

Bejeweled

Laura Tanner Swinand, Laura Tanner Jewelry

When you love doing something, it's hard to leave it behind for long. For Laura Tanner Swinand, that's designing delicate drop earrings, beaded chains, and bangle bracelets of sparkling gemstones such as druzy, labradorite, and moonstone – wrapped in silver and gold. She's the founder of the eponymous Laura Tanner Jewelry (lauratannerjewelry.com), which she launched in 2006, based in Evanston, Illinois.

"As far back as I can remember, I've loved creating tiny things by hand, whether little furniture for my dollhouse, intricate clothes for my paper dolls, or jewelry," says Swinand, 50. "I started making jewelry as a teenager, at first because I needed to customize my own earrings with clip-on backs before my parents allowed me to get my ears pierced."

In high school, her favorite classes were metalsmithing and enameling. And she brazenly peddled her designs to local stores in her hometown of Santa Barbara, California.

She comes by her love of art and design honestly. "I was always doing art projects and going to gallery openings and museum exhibitions with my mom, who's an artist," she says. After earning degrees in art history – a bachelor's from the University of Pennsylvania and a master's at the University of Southern California – Swinand held a variety of jobs at museums writing educational materials and creating youth arts programs.

Marriage and child rearing put her jewelry-making time on hold. But when her twins, now 19, started elementary school, it was time to get back into the studio. "I realized that it was what I really enjoyed doing," she says.

She turned the corner, though, at a holiday crafts show she put on with a bunch of artsy pals back in 2005. "I was blown away by the response from customers," she says. She was off and running. Her start-up capital was a $25,000 small-business loan, which she divvied up between paying a techie to build a website for her, materials to use for her creations, and packaging supplies.

In the early days, Swinand would trek to the attic in her home to make her jewelry, and only sold items sporadically at craft shows nearby. But word of mouth picked up, and she found herself barely able to fill customer orders. "I realized I either had to commit to doing this full time and hire more help," she says, "or accept that it was a hobby."

She dug down and made the commitment. She hired two assistants and rented a workshop outside her home. One mistake was trying to please everyone. "I wanted to offer everything and every color, so everybody could find something that they liked," she recalls. "As a result, I was over-purchasing. I was all over the place." In time, she reined it in and now offers only a handful of stones and colors.

For Swinand, the really tough part of being a business owner is selling. For starters, the place to land the big customers is at the large expo shows, such as the One of a Kind show, held twice a year at the Chicago Merchandise Mart, which features around 600 independent artists. That requires quite a bit of planning and legwork to set up an eye-catching booth, featuring handcrafted necklaces, earrings, bracelets, and rings. And physically, it's demanding to be on your feet for hours, days in a row, hawking your designs with a smile to potential shop owners and wholesale buyers. "It can be crazy, but I do whatever it takes to get things done," says Swinand, "I wear a lot of hats, but I love the times I spend with customers I meet at these events. Nothing compares to meeting in person and for buyers to see and touch the quality of my designs."

Roughly 50 boutiques across the country carry her jewelry, and overall sales more than doubled between 2013 and 2017. For 2018, revenues – which are split evenly between online retail sales and wholesale accounts – easily exceeded $250,000. Meantime, she turned a profit for the fifth year in a row.

Retail prices for her designs range from a pair of silver drop earrings for $28 up to $400. A point of pride: her business is environmentally friendly. All of the metal scraps are recycled. Gift boxes and bags are made from recycled content, and she uses U.S.-based suppliers, often local, to reduce her carbon footprint.

"What I make is not revolutionary," Swinand says. "There's tons of jewelry out there that has similarities to mine. I'm using traditional material, but my mission is to provide personalized service and to make the highest-quality jewelry at an affordable price, so a woman can put it on, wear it every day, and even share it with her daughter."

Making It Work

I asked Laura to look back and share her thoughts on her shift to starting her own jewelry business after being a stay-at-home mom.

Kerry: What did starting your own business mean to you personally?

Laura: Starting my own business was very meaningful to me, as it gave me an outlet for my creative interests and also an opportunity to learn new skills like running an e-commerce site, developing a wholesale business, and also direct-to-consumer sales.

Were you confident that you were doing the right thing? Any second-guessing?

I was not always confident that I was doing the right thing, but it was the right fit for me at the time, with two kids at home and a husband (at that time) who was traveling for work much of the time. It definitely has worked for me to be able to make my own schedule and work around my kids and family whenever possible.

Anything you would have done differently?

Have a business plan. I definitely started without a plan, and that made things harder. Also I held myself back in the business by dragging things out because I wanted them to be perfect. I've learned by putting it out there, even if it's not perfect, there is much more momentum in that.

Nothing is ever going to be exactly how you want it to be. You have to learn to let go and delegate and realize that you are not going to be able to do it all yourself. Giving employees more responsibility allows me to focus on the creative and long-term planning part of things.

Streamline. Don't try to please everybody. I was so seduced by different gemstones and metals. I wanted to offer everything and every color, so everybody could find something that they liked. As a result, I was over-purchasing. I was all over the place. In the last two years, I've decreased my inventory and narrowed my line down from 20 stones and colors to five and have eliminated a lot of options. I looked at my sales and realized this is what people want. This is what people are buying.

How big a role did financial rewards play in your decision?

Running this business has always been more about creativity, flexibility, and independence than financial rewards.

How do you measure your success?

The biggest reward has been that I've been able to keep it going for all of these years, and it's growing. Meantime, I'm able to provide employment to two people and to create a product that is something that provides pleasure to people and helps them feel and look better ... and makes them happy. That's pretty gratifying because it's something that puts good energy out there in the world.

What do you tell other people who ask for your advice?

Make sure that not only do you really love making jewelry (or any other handmade product), but that you have a solid understanding of what it takes to transform a hobby into a business. As I said before, I would also recommend writing a business plan going into it, no matter how small; your plan can be pretty basic and is a constantly evolving document.

Decide what you can afford to outsource or delegate, and then focus on the things you do well and that motivate you. The first few years, I did my own bookkeeping and tax preparation, but I realized that even with a small business, there was enough going on to warrant outside assistance. It was also a huge time and energy drain, which took me away from what I loved to do – design and make jewelry, market my products, and work with my wholesale and retail customers.

How to Hire Employees Wisely

One of the toughest things for a small-business owner to do is to hire employees. I have a strong personal connection to the topic. Even with my one-woman media company, the decision to bring on a summer intern, or someone to help manage social media, is excruciating for two reasons: cash flow and control. I never have been able to make that leap.

But sometimes, bringing on a part-time helper or staffer is essential for your business to succeed and grow. Not asking for help is one area where entrepreneurs can get hung up, Rebecca Barnes-Hogg, author of *The YOLO Principle: The Ultimate Hiring Guide for Small Business*, told me when I interviewed her for my Next Avenue column.

"Entrepreneurs often feel they have to be superwoman or man and do everything," she says. "After all, they are usually highly successful and often creative people. They tend to believe they can do everything themselves. That makes delegating difficult."

And for many 50+ business owners, adding staff is more than a cold-eyed business decision. Older entrepreneurs tend to be emotionally tied to or invested in their businesses, Barnes-Hogg said. "That's a good thing when creating your product or service. When it comes to hiring, we want the people we hire to make that same emotional investment. The problem becomes how to identify whether a prospective employee will share that emotional tie."

If you're considering adding staff, here's some smart advice from Barnes-Hogg:

> **Kerry:** *What do first-time entrepreneurs, especially those in their 50s and 60s, do wrong when it comes to hiring?*
>
> Rebecca Barnes-Hogg: Most entrepreneurs have no idea how much they should delegate. I recommend writing down everything you do, and I mean everything. Then go through that list with an eagle eye and cross off everything that doesn't produce revenue and could be done by someone else. This is an eye-opening moment.
>
> Another stumbling block is approaching hiring like it's a field of dreams – post a job ad and the perfect candidate will come.
>
> Job boards are decreasing in effectiveness, while referrals are increasing. That means working your networks to find connections and build relationships with prospective candidates.
>
> It also means approaching hiring like marketing. You need to show why people would want to work for you and not for another company. Job seekers today want to know the impact and value of the work they do.
>
> *Is hiring harder for business owners who have had corporate careers?*
>
> It can be even more difficult. They learn a hiring system from the company in which they worked and try to replicate it in their business. You need to create your own system.

What's your advice about how to do it right?

I have four principles: clarity, culture, communication, and consistency. The most important is clarity, and it's the hardest piece. If you want to avoid costly hiring mistakes, spend time defining your needs and wait to hire the best person rather than hiring quickly to relieve pain. Often when you take time to clarify your needs, you realize what you thought you needed and what you actually need is very different. The example I use in my book is the woman entrepreneur who thought she needed a receptionist when in fact she needed a salesperson who could also do administrative work.

How can you know when it's time to hire someone?

When the cost of doing the work yourself outweighs the cost of paying someone else to perform the tasks. While you can certainly fix your website or schedule your social media posts, does it make sense for you to spend your time doing that? Or is it more important that you do only the things you can do, like networking and building a pipeline of business?

Paying someone $10 or $15 an hour for work that takes you away from generating thousands of dollars in business makes more sense. You need to hire someone and that can be in the form of a virtual assistant, a freelancer, a project-based consultant, or a part-time or full-time employee. Today, hiring someone is more flexible than ever before.

What's the best way to negotiate pay versus benefits and flexibility for the employee?

According to Jobvite's 2018 Job Seeker Nation Study, nearly a third of jobseekers (32%) would even be willing to take a 10% pay cut for a job they're more interested in or passionate about. That's a huge opportunity to emphasize factors other than pay as part of your hiring strategy.

I advise clients that honesty is best. Provide your candidates with a realistic picture of what the job entails and what it's like working at your company. Resist the temptation to omit or gloss over the less attractive parts of the job.

In every aspect of your hiring process, communicate what you can offer. Examples might be growth and development opportunities, the ability to work closely with leadership, interesting projects, flexibility to do things differently, and work-life integration that allows work and personal life to combine and become more effective. When you do this, you'll find that negotiating with your prospective employees is easier because you've set expectations from the beginning.

Chapter Recap

In this chapter, we learned how a stay-at-home mom was able to launch a crafts-based business in incremental stages by starting it out of her home. And we discussed the importance of smart hiring decisions and knowing when it's the right time to delegate.

YOUR TO-DO LIST

- Write down in your journal thoughts on what activities you are passionate about. Is there something from your childhood that you always loved to do? Is it something you'd like to try your hand at again? The final fear, according to Patricia DiVecchio, the business and work coach who we met in Chapter 4, is what she calls door number three – the fear that when you really start the internal digging to find your passion, you're not going to find anything there. That's when you may need help from friends, colleagues, and family to trigger your memories.
- Do a Web search to see what kinds of businesses operate in your craft area locally.
- Dig into the numbers. Do you think you could monetize it? What do your potential competitors charge for their goods and services? Do they operate out of an actual office or storefront, or is it an e-business that's home based?
- Drill down to see what skills, education, and certificates the owners of those potential competitors have. Do you need to add some new competencies to your wheelhouse?

CHAPTER 6

Scooting Ahead

Tim Juntgen (r), Carolina Fun Machines

The Carolina Fun Machines showroom, located in Matthews, North Carolina, looks like a sparkling toy store with rows of tangerine, cherry-red, and purple scooters lined up.

Shop owner Tim Juntgen, 66, is slowly rolling one of those shiny two-wheelers out the front door and into the parking lot for a potential customer to take a test spin (carolinafunmachines.com/store-pictures).

His smile and low-key banter say it all. This guy loves his job. "I have never met anyone who has walked in that door that I can't make friends with," Juntgen says. "I take good care of my customers, and I build friendships with them."

Once a salesman, always a salesman. Back in 1973, Juntgen snapped up his first sales job working for IBM in Chicago. And for 35 years, he rode the fast-changing computer climate, ultimately peddling business products ranging from minicomputers to PCs to software.

Today, the one-time sales executive still relishes a sale, but he has redeployed his pitch. He's pushing Chinese-made scooters, ranging in price from $1,000 to $5,000, along with go-karts, dirt bikes, and all-terrain vehicles (ATVs). And he sells hundreds of them each year.

In 2008, Juntgen started Carolina Fun Machines (carolinafunmachines.com) as an antidote to the boredom he was battling after retiring from his $150,000-a-year software sales position. His wife, Linda, now 59, was still working full time as a high school French teacher, and he was itching to find something to do that he really loved.

It all started innocently when Linda mentioned that she wanted to try riding a scooter the two miles from their home to her job each day to save on gas. Since he had some time on his hands, he volunteered to do the shopping.

It was in his wheelhouse. Juntgen started riding mini-bikes as a kid in tiny Monticello, Indiana. "I've been a motorcycle guy all my life," he said. "I used to put about 7,000 miles a year on my Kawasaki Concours motorcycle rolling north from Charlotte to Thunder Bay, Canada, or Bar Harbor, Maine, or south to Key West."

Juntgen tapped into online scooter forums to chat with scooter owners about quality and scooter vendors. Then he visited several of the local dealers. It was while doing those estimated 500 hours of research that Juntgen saw there was a need in the marketplace for a quality mid-range-priced scooter that came with a warranty and was sold by a shop that could handle service and repairs.

"The mechanic would be me," Juntgen says. "My love of mechanics came early on." As a kid, he spent summers working on boat engines for a waterski show at a large amusement park called Indiana Beach on Lake Schaffer near his home and at a local marina. "For a long time, I thought I wanted to be a mechanic," he recalls.

"Finally, I realized I could do this business. I could afford to do it and thought I would have a lot of fun," he recalls. "I said to Linda, I know what I want to do, and you'll also get a great price on your scooter."

Juntgen's initial investment of $50,000 was spent on the purchase of 20 scooters and a retail-based computer system for his shop. No borrowing for the frugal Juntgen; he tapped his cash savings accounts. The first year, his goal was to sell 100 scooters. He sold 130.

For the first two years that the shop was up and running, though, he didn't pay himself a dime. But the frugal Juntgens and their two kids, now 18 and 22, managed to live off savings and Linda's $45,000 salary.

Five years ago, Juntgen and his wife bought the 7,600-square-foot building that garages Carolina Fun Machines for $450,000. The pair ponied up $40,000 and borrowed $410,000 via a 15-year loan at a rate of 3.4% from a local bank. "We doubled our office and showroom space, and we're building equity in the building. I paid my landlord a total of $180,000 in rent over five years. I wish I had it back," he says.

Today, the shop, which sells scooters primarily made by Chinese manufacturer Znen, has revenues of around $762,000, and the business is solidly in the black. Juntgen rolls the net profits back into the business and pays himself a base salary of $60,000. He also allots himself a bonus of $30,000 to $40,000 each year, depending on how the business does.

Why does he need all that space? To house the larger ATVs and utility task vehicles that sell in the range of $3,000 to $6,000 apiece. "That's where the demand is coming from," he says.

His secret to success: no borrowing. "When I started the business, if I didn't have the cash to buy the scooters, go-karts and such, then I didn't buy. So, if nothing is happening here, then nothing happens here. It is not the end of the world."

His one regret? He had to sell his beloved Kawasaki. "I didn't have time to ride it. But I would occasionally ride a scooter the four-and-a-half miles home from the office – just for fun."

Until this spring, that is. Juntgen bought a new blue Honda CTX700 motorcycle. "After all these years, I have the business to where I don't have to be there all the time," he says with a grin.

Making It Work

I asked Tim to look back and share his thoughts on his shift to starting his scooter business after a successful sales career.

Kerry: What did starting your own business mean to you personally?

Tim: That I could do it. Job security and building equity for the future for Linda and the kids.

Were you confident that you were doing the right thing?

For the most part. That is why I limited what we could lose.

Any second-guessing?

No.

Anything you would have done differently?

Done it sooner.

How do you measure your success?

Growth and profitability.

How big a role did financial rewards play in your decision?

Well, I did not want to work for free, and I was not looking to make millions. I thought if I enjoyed what I did and could make 60K per year, that would be okay.

How did your preparation help you succeed?

It helped us get off to a good start. What I learned in the next three years is what allowed us to reach $977K revenue in 2015 and a $995K revenue number in 2016. With the construction of the new Monroe Expressway toll road in front of our business over the last two years, our revenue numbers dropped back to $762k in 2017, and it looks like it will be about the same again this year. The new expressway is now open, so it will be interesting to see what the numbers look like next year.

What do you tell other people who ask for your advice?

Do what you love, for you will do it for a long time. Understand the income and expenses of what you want to do and if the net will be enough to keep you interested and motivated.

What are some of the unexpected rewards and surprises?

Over the last 10 years, the business has paid me $480,000 and generated an additional $457,000 in net profit. We had a CPA firm that specializes in valuing business look at the business and they recommended a sale price of

$500,000. Along with that, we have paid off the building with the help of the state when they purchased part of our parking lot for the expressway. They gave us just under $300,000, which we used to pay down the note. We have one payment left, so the building will be paid off this year, and it has a value of around $600,000.

Is this what I had in mind back in 2008? Not really. I was just looking for something to do until Linda retired in five years. Linda stayed teaching for 10 years. Our daughter was in her French class, and she wanted to teach until Emily graduated. Emily graduated this year and is now in college at NC State.

Linda retired as a North Carolina teacher and took her pension after 35 years in June. She lasted one month before she went crazy, and took a French teaching position in Ft. Mill, South Carolina. Being empty nesters and wanting a house with a master bedroom downstairs, we are in the process of building a new home in South Carolina that will make the commute more equal for the two of us.

What was the biggest challenge?

What was and still is the biggest challenge relates to finding and keeping exceptional employees. Today with unemployment being at historic low levels, it's the biggest challenge my business faces.

Financing Your Start-Up

Your first step is to draw up a personal budget to find places you can trim back your spending. Optional expenses like travel and meals out are clear cuts. One possibility for lowering your monthly nut is to downsize to a smaller home or condo. Another is to refinance your mortgage to a lower rate. Then, beginning at least two years before your launch, pay down any outstanding non-mortgage debt, from credit card balances to auto loans.

Set aside savings to carry you through some potential lean days in your early days. A year's worth of living expenses is ideal because you may have to tap into those funds.

And when you're trying to get a bead on how much you will need for start-up costs, it's always good to overestimate. Many people who take the entrepreneurship route think they will make more income initially than they probably will, and lowball their start-up costs. Little wonder that half of all new small businesses fail within five years, according to the Small Business Administration.

So at least two years before you plan to launch, get a clear picture of what a start-up will cost you and then begin to line up your potential sources of financing.

To get a frank valuation of your likely expenses, consult with the free resources accessible to you. One is SCORE, an organization of experienced businesspeople who volunteer their expertise to entrepreneurs that I've mentioned before. The SBA and AARP also provide online educational resources and webinars to help develop a business plan, among other start-up needs.

"It's a good idea to pull together an airtight budget," says Edward Rogoff, dean at LIU Brooklyn, School of Business, Public Administration, and Information Sciences. "Then add a cushion of 20% to your upfront costs to be on the safe side."

Financing a mid-life or retiree start-up can be problematic. The most common method is using personal savings, says Rogoff. That can be risky and pricey, given the rules governing withdrawals from retirement accounts.

But entrepreneurs can also pursue local economic development loans or perhaps use crowdfunding sites to raise capital. "Generally, as a person gets old, their tolerance for risk decreases, or it should decrease," Rogoff says. "Somebody who is 26 and starting a business can bet the ranch because if it fails, at 31, they can start another business. But somebody who is 61 or 68 who starts a business can't bet the ranch because at 75 or older, they won't be able to get the ranch back and start over."

There are a variety of practical approaches, Rogoff says. A retiree might find a partner to chip in, or start small – with a website, for example, rather than a bricks-and-mortar store.

In addition to dipping into personal savings accounts, another common route for older entrepreneurs is calling on the generosity of friends and family.

For many who want to start a business, the local bank is frequently a first stop for financing. But "most banks aren't that keen on loans for a senior business start-up, because they are not big enough," says

Elizabeth Isele, a founder of the Global Institute for Experienced Entrepreneurship (experieneurship.com). For those who get through the gatekeepers, a solid business plan and a clean credit record are preconditions. And a lender probably will want the borrower to be prepared to personally invest in the business.

"Banks don't like to lend money for ideas," Rogoff says. "They lend money against cash flow for existing businesses and against assets they can collect against in the future." One resource for learning more is USA.gov/business, the federal government's site for entrepreneurs seeking small-business loans.

For those who have built up some equity in their homes, a home equity loan is a fairly stress-free route to gain access to cash, and interest is usually manageable. Even faster is using personal credit cards. "But however tempting that is, it's very expensive," Rogoff says.

Another option is to seek out so-called angel investors who will back you in exchange for equity or partial ownership. The SBA's Small Business Investment Company program can offer leads. In general, the best way to find an angel investor is for up-and-coming business proprietors to contact the network they developed during their careers, Rogoff says.

A new twist is "rollovers as business start-ups," or ROBS, which raise the risks a bit higher, according to some experts. With this approach, business owners use their retirement funds, like 401(k) assets, to finance or expand a business without incurring taxes or penalties. The account is rolled over into a new retirement fund. And that new retirement fund, in effect, becomes a shareholder in the start-up. It's legitimate, according to the Internal Revenue Service, but it's complex. And if it is not set up perfectly, it could result in penalties and a big tax bill.

THE NITTY-GRITTY ON START-UP FUNDS

Savings. Most start-ups are backed with personal savings. (This is where a severance package comes in handy.) It's advisable to set aside at least six months of fixed living expenses, though. Try not to dip into your retirement savings – you'll be subject to withdrawal penalties and income taxes and lose the tax-deferred compounding that could serve you well in retirement.

(*Continued*)

THE NITTY-GRITTY ON START-UP FUNDS (*Cont'd*)

Friends and relatives. They often lend money at low or no interest. Be sure to put the terms in writing so that there are no misunderstandings about interest and repayment. And be forewarned: Money can wreak havoc on relationships should things not work out as planned. Tread lightly if you think it might have the possibility of turning ugly.

Banks and credit unions. A solid business plan and a shiny credit record are prerequisites. You might try a bank that's familiar with you or your industry, or one that is active in small-business lending. To find a bank that offers SBA-guaranteed loans, check the "Local Resources" section of the agency's website (sba.gov). An SBA-guaranteed bank loan can keep your down payment and monthly payments low. Keep in mind that a lender will still want you to put up collateral, usually in the form of a real estate asset. Plan to have some capital or equity that you personally put into the business. Lenders want you to have some skin in the game, so to speak. Business.usa.gov is the federal government's site for entrepreneurs seeking short-term microloans and small-business loans. Search this site for info on all programs available in your state.

Angel investors and venture capital firms. These invest in exchange for equity or partial ownership. But they are typically overwhelmed by requests for financing. Another source of venture capital is the SBA's Small Business Investment Company Program.

Economic development programs. This type of financing will take a little footwork, but it's worth pursuing. For example, if you're a woman, you might consider getting your firm certified as a woman-owned business. That can help you qualify for money that's only available to companies with that designation.

Certifications. Certifications can also help you land government clients. Small-business certifications and verifications confirm a company's status, like whether the principal owner is a minority group member or the firm is located in an economically disadvantaged area. The SBA's economic development department can help you determine if this might be an avenue for you. If you're a veteran, the Department of Veterans Affairs, for instance, can provide you with information on how to get certified.

Grants. Grants.gov lists information on more than 1,000 federal grant programs. Female entrepreneurs should check out the SBA network of nearly 100 Women's Business Centers around the country. They offer state, local, and private grant information to women interested in starting for-profit or nonprofit businesses.

Online seed money. Virtual fundraising campaigns on sites like Kickstarter, Indiegogo, and GoFundMe have been gaining in acceptance with people raising money for a pet project or new business. But if you're trying to crowdfund money this way, you'll need savvy marketing and elbow grease to create a winner.

Entrepreneurs use Kickstarter, the largest crowdfunding website, to find people who'll invest small amounts of money in tech projects or creative endeavors like music or video games. Someone can donate anywhere from $1 to the sky's the limit. It's not an investment. Most successfully funded projects on Kickstarter raise under $10,000.

Each of the big crowdfunding sites handles the funding process differently. On Kickstarter, when people donate, their credit cards are charged. Once you reach your goal, Kickstarter takes 5% of the amount raised, and you pay 3 to 5% for credit card processing. If you don't bring in all the money you set as your goal by the deadline, the pledges are canceled, contributors aren't charged, and Kickstarter takes nothing.

Indiegogo charges a 5% fee on the funds you raise, plus you pay 3% for credit card or PayPal processing. Unlike Kickstarter, pledges aren't canceled if you don't reach your goal.

GoFundMe.com deducts a 5% fee and a 3% processing fee from each donation. All the remaining money you collect goes directly to you.

Crowdlending is a variation on the theme, but in this case, people expect to get their money back. For example, Chancey M. Lindsey-Peake, 62, a retired housekeeper and nanny, started her banana bread bakery, Banana Manna (bananamanna.com), in Greenville, South Carolina. Her backing: a $5,000 zero-interest loan funded through Kiva (kiva.org), a nonprofit micro-lending company in San Francisco, that she fully repaid. Kiva patches together multiple lenders to fund loans as small as $25, and serves borrowers in more than 82 countries.

Home equity loans. This may be an option because the funds are usually taken as a lump sum that you can pay off over time. If you have equity in your home and a credit score well above 700, it may be worth exploring. Consult a financial adviser. Just be certain that you'll be able to repay this kind of financing – your house is on the line.

And now the two sources of money you really don't want to use:

Credit cards. Avoid using plastic at all costs. Most cards carry double-digit interest rates, which is an outlandish price to pay for starting a business. Also, it's very easy to get yourself into trouble this way, given the financial ups and downs of a new venture.

Retirement savings. Trust me, you don't want to dip into your 401(k) or IRA. Not only will you owe income taxes by taking money out, you'll lose the tax-deferred compounding and, if you're younger than 59½, you'll owe IRS withdrawal penalties. Worst of all, you'll hijack your future financial security. Please don't do that. No business is worth it.

Chapter Recap

In this chapter, we learned how a retiree was able to redeploy his salesmanship skills with a deep passion for motorcycles and mechanics to create a niche business. Deep market research and no borrowing helped him gain traction in the early years. We also learned about various sources for funding a start-up.

YOUR TO-DO LIST

- Write down in your journal what kinds of activities you loved as a child. Is there a business concept hidden there or a path for self-employment?
- Research what the costs might be to launch a home-based business.
- Run the numbers and do a thorough analysis of your personal sources of funding.
- Ask yourself: How many years until you really plan to retire? Does the business concept have time to grow and prosper?

CHAPTER 7

Write Stuff

Amy Bass, Nota Bene

In 2007, Pittsburgh stay-at-home mom Evvy Diamond found herself getting restless. With two of her three sons college bound, she felt it was time for her to earn an income.

Meanwhile, her friend Amy Bass, a VP at a small Pittsburgh money-management firm, was facing a mid-life crisis after two decades in the business: "As I approached 50, I decided I could no longer work for someone else. I needed to own something," Bass recalls.

In time, the two friends' ambitions would connect.

As Diamond contemplated what to do, she remembered her love of notepaper. "Even as a child, I would save the last piece of stationery of every set because I didn't want to part with it," she says. Motivated by the memory, she shelled out $1,000 to purchase a century-old cast-iron letterpress from a printing shop in nearby Duquesne, Pennsylvania, that was closing.

The singular press, which weighs a ton, was hauled by an auto transporter to her home and set up in the garage. She painstakingly restored it by canvassing flea markets to buy vintage dies. And then she taught herself how to manually print by reading blogs and poring through books on the art of letterpress printing.

Before long, she was hand-coloring cards and lining the envelopes. Painting and illustration had been Diamond's creative pursuits since she was a teenager. Within a few months, she was peddling a card line, featuring her designs, by word of mouth.

Buoyed by the response from friends, Diamond rented a booth at the 2007 Stationery Show in New York. It was time to go prime time. "I thought, 'Let me try,'" Diamond says. "I went alone, and it was so exciting."

It paid off. She landed an order of 600 Christmas cards from a Cross Pen store in Boston. She painstakingly printed and cut the paper, and hand-colored and lined all the envelopes, for each one.

Then she thought she got her big break: 5,000 cards for a prestigious New York shop. Only that $12,500 order was canceled before she got paid – and she was left holding the cards. "I knew I could sell them, but it wasn't going to happen out of my garage."

Within weeks, she signed a lease for a 400-square-foot retail space in the Aspinwall neighborhood of Pittsburgh, and opened a boutique called Nota Bene (notabenepaper.com) to sell made-to-order bespoke stationery, both her own and others ("Nota Bene" means "note well.")

"I was so down, and a friend who also runs a shop in Aspinwall had told me that a 400-square-foot space was going to be available," she recalls. "I signed the lease without even having a business plan."

Diamond's initial $20,000 investment went toward rent, paper, album samples, and fixing up the retail space. She tapped savings from sales generated by her home-based business, along with a line of credit and credit cards.

Soon Bass began lending a hand after work, waiting on customers and helping with the books in her spare time and on weekends, while she worked full time at the money-management firm.

Bass found herself smitten with the work. And Diamond quickly realized she needed her friend's business savvy. So a year after

Diamond opened the shop, they struck a deal: Bass invested $25,000 and signed on as full-time partner. The pay Bass gave up to work for Nota Bene: six figures.

"I went through a mid-life crisis – my husband tells me it would have been cheaper to buy a sports car – but at approaching 50, I decided that I needed to run a business, work in a small-town setting near my home, and be creative," Bass says.

Diamond's transformation into the owner-operator of a fast-growing business is one that many stay-at-home moms fantasize about. She pulled it off in no small part due to 60-hour work weeks, a knack for customer-service, and a flair for design.

Diamond unabashedly states that the shop's overall success is due in large measure to Bass.

"We were like two pieces of a puzzle," Diamond says. Bass brings management skills ranging from bookkeeping and tech expertise to scheduling and buying inventory.

Of course, the competition from digital do-it-yourselfers and on-line shopfronts, such as Etsy and Tinyprints, has been lurking from the earliest days. "To say I was uncertain of the outcome of Nota Bene is an understatement," Diamond says.

The shop makes most of its sales – on track to exceed $700,000 in 2019 – from wedding invitations. But the women found a niche with in-house printing to personalize notecards from vendors like Crane and William Arthur. And it stocks items like calendars, candles, and baby gifts, which get people into the store more regularly. "We found people were coming in for invitations and buying gifts," Bass says.

About two years ago, Diamond retired, "mostly for personal reasons," says Bass. "She still has a son at home, and the store has really grown and required too much of her time, so I am now the sole owner."

What does Nota Bene do best? "It all comes down to a commitment to unparalleled customer service. In a world of emails and Evites, there is a stronger need than ever for the look and feel of handwritten note, unique gift, or personal invitation," Bass says.

Nota Bene has plenty of online competition in these areas, but people still want the personal connection. Same goes for the owner. Bass says the greatest reward is when a happy client says, "Oh, my gosh, I need to give you a hug."

Making It Work

I asked Amy to look back and share her thoughts on her shift to the stationery business.

> **Kerry: What did starting your own business with Evvy mean to you personally?**

Amy: To me it meant no longer working for anyone else. It meant the ability to own and create something of my own and then being directly rewarded for my hard work. I was also able to be creative and involved in all aspects of a business: design, marketing, finance, customer service, social media, etc.

> **Were you confident that you were doing the right thing? Any second-guessing?**

No, scared to death – giving up a big salary and starting something brand new. But no regrets!

> **Anything you would have done differently?**

I don't think I would have done anything differently.

> **How do you measure your success?**

Well, still in business 10 years later, in the world of emails and Evites. Also, financially we are doing great. Sales have grown tremendously, mostly in the invitation business, and we have developed a great reputation.

> **How big a role did financial rewards play in your decision?**

I think in my case it was quite the opposite, it was more of a deterrent, but thankfully it all worked out.

> **How did your preparation help you succeed?**

Regarding preparation, I didn't do any. I jumped right in. Evvy had started it, but we never had a business plan or prepared for how big it would become.

What do you tell other people who ask for your advice?

When people ask for advice or say, "I would love to open a store," I say it isn't as easy or as fun as it looks. It takes a lot of time and hard work and can be stressful.

What books did you find helpful?

Unfortunately, I didn't read any books, but probably should have.

What are some of the unexpected rewards and surprises?

Rewards: Financial has been unexpected. The customer feedback has been wonderful; the relationships you develop with them are so special. Every time someone walks in and tells you the store is beautiful is a reward. Sometimes it's the little things, the small compliments that make your day.

What was the biggest challenge?

The challenges have been trying not to make mistakes either by our store or vendors, ultimately keeping the customers happy – it's a daily challenge. But we learn from our mistakes and keep getting better. Other challenges: Employees – work schedules, how they treat customers, and training. Plus, how to market our store in the world of social media and compete with the internet – our biggest competitor.

CREATING A WINNING PARTNERSHIP

A successful partnership takes careful advance planning and regular checkups.

Start by asking, "Why a partner?" The answer might be it's someone who can bring in the capital, or a skill set, or expertise you lack, as in the case of Bass and Diamond. Don't take this decision lightly. In reality, it might be far simpler and cheaper to hire someone on a contract basis who can fill the need.

(Continued)

CREATING A WINNING PARTNERSHIP (*Cont'd*)

Get to know your prospective partner. Understand his or her personal and professional ethics, views, and goals. If you can't show your true colors and vice versa before you go into partnership, you're in trouble. You need to be comfortable, at ease with each other, and honest. No pulling punches. The great thing about Bass and Diamond is they had a friendship first, then developed a working relationship over time. Diamond offered a helping hand for nearly a year before the two decided to create an official partnership.

If you don't have this situation or have not worked together in the past, you might start with a trial period and take on one project or client or work side by side for a set time frame, to see how your work personalities jibe before making a formal commitment. This is also a great way to learn about each other's character and core values.

Approach the potential pairing as a job interview of each other. Interview former colleagues and people he or she has managed and worked alongside of, and talk to personal references such as family members or friends, if appropriate, to glean if there's a good fit between the two of you.

Look for a dance partner who's different from you. Seek out a partner who complements your skills and adds an ingredient you don't have. For example, at Nota Bene, Diamond was the primary creative force, and Bass brought the financial chops.

Networking can help you find your counterpart. Do you know anyone you've met at an industry conference who might be interested in teaming up? There are online chat groups and blogs geared to and for entrepreneurs, and also so-called matchmaking sites such as CoFoundersLab.com, Founders-Nation.com, and StartupWeekend.org. Your alma mater or a nearby local college or university might also be a treasure trove of contacts for you, particularly if they have a business school or incubator for entrepreneurs.

Establish ground rules. You want to avoid having any resentments if one partner has misunderstood the specific roles each will play. Set clear boundaries, duties, and expectations.

Hire a lawyer and an accountant. You'll need pros to put together an official written partnership agreement. Elements to establish: what percentage of the business each of you owns, how much capital you each will contribute, salaries, what will happen if one of you wants to leave the partnership, and detailed roles and responsibilities.

With a start-up, you both may agree to postpone compensation for a set time or until the business attains a certain revenue threshold. If one of you will be working more hours than the other, that should be a consideration when it comes to setting salaries. There can be clauses to adjust these agreements at different time intervals.

Importantly, you should have a written understanding of what happens if one of you wants to leave the business, or you both decide to shut down the shop. For example, if one person wants out, consider agreeing upon a percentage of the business's value for which each partner can be bought out.

Talk, talk, talk. Regular daily meetings and open lines of communication are nonnegotiable. Quarterly financial reviews and outlooks are essential.

Never forget this is business, not pleasure. Going into a partnership with a dear friend or a family member, even a spouse, can be tricky. If the business or the working relationship sours, you not only lose a friend, but you damage a family bond as well, and that's hard to fix.

From the partnerships I've studied, the original idea for a business generally comes from one person, as it did with Diamond. But once she got up and running, she realized that she only had so much time and could really use help with the financial end of things to keep the business on track and growing. The secret sauce ingredient to their success: trust.

Chapter Recap

In this chapter, we learned how it can take two to support a business. Sharing the risk, capital infusion, and the ups and downs can be a genuine lifeline for a small business. With the proper preparation, when each partner brings their own unique talents to create a whole, it can be a winning combination.

YOUR TO-DO LIST

- In your journal, create a job sketch for your ideal partner.
- Write down your strengths and weaknesses – both hard and soft skills – and what a partner would need to bring to fill those gaps.
- Spend time considering how you might work on a daily basis with a partner. What would that look like and feel like?
- Do some deep-dive soul-searching. Are you truly willing to share your business with someone else? Your dream? Your passion?

CHAPTER

Horsing Around

Dragonfly Woodworks Display

For Joan Sadler, the childhood memory of her parents taking her to Virginia Beach for pony rides at the carnival makes her beam. "We'd go round and round and around," Sadler says. "I was five years old, and I was crazy about ponies."

Today, Sadler, 59, carves wooden flower planters adorned with the sculpted heads of ponies, among other equestrian-themed items, such as saddle and bridle racks and tack trunks. She hones her craft in a cozy woodshop tucked inside her home's garage in Gaetna, Virginia, a tiny town of around 1,250 residents about 50 miles from Roanoke.

From there, she hits the road throughout the year to attend horse shows in the southeast. That's where she peddles her hand-hewn designs. Sadler's Dragonfly Woodworks display is typically tucked under a tree alongside the rings of brightly painted jumps. It's a buzzy meeting spot for trainers, competitors, owners, and grooms, who might grab a seat on one of her large wooden tack trunks to chat, admire her goods, and place custom orders.

"This is heaven. I get to sit here in my chair and watch the most beautiful horses walk by all day long," she says. "It's a carnival. It's like the one I went to as a kid. It's that high-energy atmosphere of excitement."

Sadler started her horse-themed woodworking business in earnest about four years ago. But her love of horses (and woodworking) runs deep. She started riding lessons at the age of 10. She skipped college, and in her 20s, earned a living breaking, galloping, and training thoroughbred racehorses.

But marriage (she has now been married for nearly four decades) and motherhood eventually intervened, and she had to step out of the tack. At the age of 38, she went back to school and earned a degree in nursing. "It was one of the coolest things I've ever done," she says. "It taught me about critical thinking and gave me a boost of confidence."

When she graduated, she accepted a position as a staff nurse at a rural Virginia medical center, but the work took its toll. "I was in the trenches, and there was such sadness, death, and dying," Sadler says.

Her anxiety and depression ratcheted up, and she turned to her tiny woodworking studio to escape. Woodworking was in her DNA. "My granddaddy was a woodworker," she says. "Woodworking for me goes way back. I can remember as a little girl walking down to the basement where he was working and how it smelled and what the shop looked like – it was a happy place for me."

Sadler began dabbling in her woodworking hobby in her 20s. "My husband gave me a table saw when we got married," she says with a laugh. "Then he built a big workbench. When a friend needed to store a band saw, I took it, and just started making things."

Her grandfather had passed away, so she taught herself as she went along. "It was difficult, a little bit hit and miss," she says with a wink.

But mostly a hit. "I felt such joy going out to my shop," she says. "It was my solitude. I would refinish people's furniture, and make small objects – just playing in it." And she regularly studied *Fine Woodworking* (finewoodworking.com) magazine for ideas, gradually giving her handiwork as gifts. When her daughter, Jess, now 36, was a child, Sadler built her a miniature stable with stalls for her Breyer (Breyerhorses.com) horse collection.

Eventually, she stepped away from nursing to help with caregiving for her three grandchildren and her mother, now 85, who moved in with her. Without the pressure of the hospital, she found herself devoting more time to her woodworking as well. "The more I did, the happier I was," Sadler says. "I learned that the best thing for me is to be creative."

It was the loss of her older sister from kidney disease in 2015, though, that pushed her to begin to sell her work. "I was devastated by her death," she says. "She was not that much older than me. I had a hard time getting up and being motivated again. I just wanted to sleep."

Sadler started shamanic journeying (the inner art of traveling to invisible worlds) as a way of communicating with her inner self and retrieve information. "I could do it immediately," she says. "I've never been a religious person. I never went to church and can't quote a Bible passage, even though I come from a long line of Baptists. But it started a spiritual path for me."

The process was life changing. "I opened up, and the message came to me that I had everything I need to find my next chapter," she says. "It came to me that I had this deep love of horses – I needed to do something horse related. And there it was – the woodworking studio. I realized that I could use this craft to connect to the horse world in an entirely different way. I can no longer ride because of my arthritis, and I don't want to teach riding, but I could go to horse shows and watch all the pretty horses and build a woodworking business in this world I loved."

Her start-up costs were minimal since she already owned the equipment and had the workspace. All she needed to buy to get going was wood – oak, birch plywood, spruce – and hardware.

To earn money to buy her supplies, she started mowing and bush-hogging fields for her neighbors. She and her husband, a Master Gardener, already had the equipment for that. "I would earn $500 at a time, and I would go out and buy a bunch of wood," she says. "The first time I went to a horse show in Lexington, Virginia, my stuff sold like hotcakes. That's when I knew I had something here."

Sadler doesn't have the funds for a marketing plan, but she has a Facebook page and her sales (items sell for anywhere from $26 to $1,000) have been doubling each year. The secret: word-of-mouth accolades shared through the horse community. Customers now regularly call her to place orders.

Caregiving duties do interrupt her taking care of business, "but that's one of the wonderful things of being your own boss," Sadler says.

Making It Work

I asked Joan to look back and share her thoughts on starting her woodworking business.

Kerry: What did starting your own business mean to you?

Joan: Freedom. You know when the personality test tells you whether you're either a circle, square, triangle, or a squiggle? I'm a squiggle.

Were you confident that you were doing the right thing? Any second-guessing?

Lots of second-guessing, but then the business kept working. I would talk to the people at the horse shows, and they would get as excited about it as I did. I never knew I could *sell*. That was a big piece of it. I get so excited about what I'm doing, and I have so many repeat customers now. It just keeps spreading.

Anything you would have done differently?

Not sit in depression for so long. I should have started journeying and praying about it a lot earlier.

Everything works out the way it's supposed to. I believe that. And who knows how long I will do this? I'm having a blast, and I am making money. But at this age, you can try different things.

How do you measure your success?

Money and happiness. My family is really proud of me. They're standing at my back. My daughter tells me all the time that she knew I could do it. She's my biggest fan, and that's magic.

How did your preparation help you succeed?

I did it in baby steps. The horse world was so engrained in me for my entire life. I did do what I wanted to do when I was younger. I knew I wanted to get married and have a family, and I did.

What do you tell other people who ask for your advice?

Don't give up. You don't quit. Do everything you can do to do what you're passionate about because that's what I have done all my life. You make the choice. It might not be perfect. But you made the choice. You are going with it. I'm muddling my way. I have learned to quit taking myself so seriously. You don't learn that until you're this age.

What was the biggest challenge?

Money. I couldn't take it out of the family coffer because we really didn't have anything for me to take. And going out on the road alone for days at a time made me anxious. Now I have a German Shepherd that I rescued, Yodi, who comes with me. She's a celebrity at the shows. People love to meet her and she keeps me calm.

Any unexpected rewards and surprises?

The family support and approval. That really surprised me. And I didn't realize how creative I was, or that I could be a salesperson. And I never thought I was comfortable talking to people. I'm more of an animal person. But my nursing days had helped me learn to be warm and friendly. I love that people often congregate at my booth. Maybe it's because I'm upbeat. I'm the cheerleader on the long days at the showgrounds.

I persevered. I feel proud of myself. It's more than just my family, or a customer, saying they love my work. It's when I am driving home after being out and selling for several days a row, and I am going "Ahh … I did it. I did it." I'm not getting rich, but my life is rich because of it. That's the good stuff.

Getting Started

Do a Test Ride

Moonlight or apprentice. A client of career consultant Maggie Mistal (maggiemistal.com) who dreamed of débuting his own bakery, and had loved to bake in his spare time, started making cookies on nights and weekends for a local bakery. Within six months, he hung up his spatula. It was too much work for too little money. He kept his day job and now just bakes for pleasure. "Don't ruin a hobby that you love," Mistal says.

I agree with her. This is one of my mantras. Simply because you have been dabbling for decades doesn't mean it will translate to a viable business. What's dreamy and your respite in your spare time can be drudgery when it's your full-time job.

That said, turning a hobby into a business *can* work, provided you give yourself the time to find how you can provide something distinctive that's not already being offered in the marketplace, and you have the financial reserves, so it has time to get its footing.

In the study "The Tortoise versus the Hare: Progress and Business Viability Differences Between Conventional and Leisure-based Founders," published in the *Journal of Business Venturing*, researchers Phillip H. Kim, Kyle C. Longest, and Stephen Lippmann found that hobby-based entrepreneurs lagged behind other founders in the first few years. But in the end, the hobby-to-business founders were more likely than others to produce revenue and a profit.

The study reports that "according to the U.S. National Federation of Independent Businesses, 22% of small-business owners reported having a hobby or special interest related to their products or services, suggesting that leisure-based entrepreneurship is a non-trivial matter.

"However, ventures that straddle the work and non-work divide often develop more casually," according to the report's authors. "Participation in serious leisure activities can provide potential entrepreneurs with knowledge of the production processes, markets, or any of a variety of other important pieces of information necessary for successful entrepreneurship. Armed with these resources, we argue leisure-based founders approach entrepreneurship in ways that do not depend on a rate-based evaluation framework, and that these business owners are driven by a different set of motives favoring slow and steady commitment to their venture."

In other words, the love of the work is what keeps you going, and the insider knowledge of being a consumer or bystander in the arena over the years permits you to discern what people really want to buy, or a service that is in demand. Makes perfect sense to me.

When we thinking of entrepreneurship, it often has a beguiled image of beginning a daring new business with daunting start-up costs and risk. But in fact, entrepreneurships can be low-key self-employment like Sadler's woodworking that, as the report says, starts "casually."

Here are a few ways to earn income from a hobby that you might begin informally to see if there's more to it for you.

Teach

You might teach a class in something that's your hobby: say, piano or guitar lessons, a foreign language, chess, or cooking. Leslie Bailey-Clark, 53, works as a commercial-lines account manager through contract work arranged by Work At Home Vintage Experts (WAHVE. com) for an insurance company in Abilene, Texas. She earns $20 an hour for 30 hours a week. At the same time, Bailey-Clarke, who lives in Covington, Georgia, is a voice coach. "I teach people as young as 4 and as old as 86 how to sing properly, or prepare for public speaking," she told me. "Actors and actresses also come to my house for coaching."

Bailey-Clarke spends several hours a week teaching and charges $30 an hour. "It is definitely more than a job," she says. "It's my passion. One of these days I will be doing this teaching as my main thing."

Your clients might arrive over the transom via word of mouth, as Bailey-Clarke's do. "I'm not interested in complete strangers coming to my home," she says. "My clients hear about me from the choir director at my church, or they hear me sing."

You could also land a teaching gig at a community college's continuing education program. You might charge for webinars or tutorials online via your website. You can post fliers in your community stores to spread the word. If your bent is music, a local musical-instrument store owner might agree to pass along the word about your services to her clientele.

Sell Merchandise to Other Aficionados

If gourmet cooking is your bailiwick, you might, for instance, import artisan pottery from Ireland. One friend who shares my equine passion, Jennifer Hedgepeth, for example, has developed a successful business selling to the horsey set via her EQ•uipe (equipequine. biz), a full-service consignment retailer offering gently used saddles, bridles, and girths.

Talk About It

If you're an expert in your pastime, show it off by delivering speeches, or writing blog posts or articles for publications both print and online. You might start a business leading tours in your town that reflect your interest. I recently heard about a rock-and-roll tour a music buff leads in New York City; he visits musician's haunts and recording studios, and weaves historical tales of the times and hijinks into his presentation. I might enjoy leading people on tours of horse farms in Virginia that have cool architecture, or famous equine residents past and present; say, Triple Crown Winners.

Check Out What Others Are Doing

Are there consultants making money in your hobby field? What are they charging? Is there someone offering tuition-based workshops both in person or online? What are their credentials? Could you offer your own spin with the right certification?

Last spring, I attended a workshop designed for those of us who compete in horse shows to help conquer our performance nerves. It was fine. A dozen of us paid $25 each for an hour discussion with the guru. I left, however, convinced that I could have presented that same material, but even better. After five decades of competing at the top horse shows in the country, I've heard much of what she had to say for years from trainers, fellow competitors, and even career coaches, who I've met in the course of my work as a work and jobs expert.

10 TIPS TO STARTING A HOME BUSINESS

Running your own business from home sounds lovely. You're your own boss and can work when and where you choose. You're not stuck with a big rent bill, and – my favorite part – you can walk your dog any time you want. I do. It clears my mind and makes for a happy dog, too.

Let's be honest, though: not all of us have the discipline and setup to make this work environment, well, work. If you're game to try, here's what you need to keep in mind to make working from home a success.

1. **Get the proper permits.** If you're operating a business out of your home, you may need tax registrations, business and occupational licenses, and permits from state and local governments. If you belong to a homeowner's association, make sure there aren't any limits to doing so. The local experts at SCORE, a nonprofit that offers free business advice, should be able to give you the lay of the land.

2. **Revise your insurance.** You probably need to add an insurance rider to your homeowner's or renter's policy to cover any incidents should a delivery person or client get injured on your property. The cost of a rider might be around $100 a year per $2,500 of additional coverage. The added rate would fluctuate by the amount of insurance you want and the volume of inventory stored at home that you'll want to protect from theft or damage.

    If you need extra coverage, you can opt for a business owners' policy – an insurance package that covers your business property and provides liability coverage for clients coming to your home. These policies generally cost from $500 to $3,500 per year.

    Each state has its own rules about insurance. The Insurance Information Institute (iii.org), an industry trade group and information clearinghouse, is a place to start your research.

3. **Don't overlook your taxes.** Pay estimated federal taxes on business income each quarter. Depending on the location of your business, you may be required to pay state and local income and business taxes, too. Go to the IRS Self-Employed Individual Tax Center (irs.gov/businesses/small-businesses-self-employed/self-employed-individuals-tax-center) to learn how to pay the federal taxes. You also may want to consult your accountant.

4. **Establish your workspace.** You should be able to take a tax deduction for 100% of expenditures directly related to your home office, such as the purchase of a work computer or printer.

(*Continued*)

10 TIPS TO STARTING A HOME BUSINESS (*Cont'd*)

The other kind of tax-deductible home office outlays are "indirect" ones that are prorated, based on the square footage of your home and office. These are things like your mortgage or rent, insurance, and utility bills.

In general, to get the write-off, the zone must be used for work entirely and on a routine basis, either as your main place of business or a place to meet with clients. To get the deduction, you must file Form 8829, "Expenses for Business Use of Your Home." For full details, go to IRS Publication 587.

In essence, if the square footage of your home office equals 10% of your home's total, you can claim 10% of its expenses.

The IRS also has a "simplified option" rule, which permits you to deduct $5 per square foot of your home office on your return, with a maximum write-off of $1,500 (based on a maximum of 300 square feet). I recommend that you snap a photo of your office space so you have a record, in case the IRS wants proof.

5. **Create a work plan.** This is a tough one for me, but it's a smart idea if you can set work hours and do your best to follow them. I personally work early mornings, but avoid evening hours. That's easier said than done, but burnout will do zilch to increase your business.

6. **Find a mentor/peer.** You will run across this tip many times in this book, but in this instance, I suggest finding a compatriot of some sort who is in your line of business and maybe working solo, too. That's because working alone can be pretty isolating, and you don't have anyone down the hall to ask for feedback or to bounce ideas off. Look for a mentor or fellow home worker among your industry friends. This relationship can take time to gel.

7. **Don't skip the human connection.** Find ways to meet clients or colleagues for coffee or a meal face to face. And attend industry conferences, seminars, and local Rotary club meetings where other small-business people hang out. At the very least, pick up the phone and talk to someone instead of texting or sending an email. It's a time zap, and I am guilty of avoiding this myself, but boy, is it ever energizing to take the time to do this one.

8. **Engage with social media.** I suggest this one with some caution. You don't want to get too distracted, but an active presence in LinkedIn groups, for example, that relate to your industry and clients is smart business. It shows your expertise and provides a sense of connection to a community. Same goes with Facebook and Twitter interactions, but keep those under control.

9. **Don't be shy about promotion.** In addition to having a LinkedIn profile, business pages on Facebook, Instagram, Pinterest, and Twitter are additional ways to spread the word. The cost is nil unless you decide to run ads. See what your competitors are using. Crafters, for example, often display their work on Instagram or Pinterest, but a Facebook page can be a great way to showcase your goods and services and build a following. LinkedIn, Twitter, and Facebook are my go-tos to draw people to my published work, and hopefully encourage them to buy my books or hire me as an expert speaker.

10. **Keep your tech skills sharp.** When you work at home, there's no tech support human to call when things go south. I have become a big fan of AppleCare. If you're a Mac user, the Genius Bar at your local Apple Store is your friend. Community colleges offer basic computer classes. YouTube videos can help with slews of stumbling blocks. LinkedIn Learning has great tutorials that might be able to solve your issues or answer questions. If you need to give presentations, you should become conversant with Web-based meeting programs such as GoToMeeting, Cisco WebEx, Join.Me, TeamViewer, or Zoom.

Chapter Recap

In this chapter, we learned the joys of starting a business at home from your hobby, but also that the path can be meandering and slow. That might be just what you're seeking. And we also discovered that these kinds of businesses can take longer to succeed than those not started from a hobby, but they often perform better over time.

YOUR TO-DO LIST

- Jot down a list of businesses that are related to your hobby.
- Consider what you might be able to add to that roster that's unique.
- Check to see if there are regulations in your town for a home-based business.
- If you have already started a side business with your hobby, investigate ways to self-promote gratis on the various social media platforms.

PART

II

BUILDING A WINNING SENIOR–
JUNIOR PARTNERSHIP

Many mid-life entrepreneurs are creating businesses alongside a younger member of their family, or a cofounder decades younger. It's a winning recipe. These intergenerational pairings are energizing and, to me, represent a great blueprint for future success.

While there are no statistics to document these new generational pairings, the trend appears to be gathering momentum. And recent studies, while not specifically about small businesses, have found intergenerational work teams to be more productive.

What I love about this start-up synergy is the older partner can bring decades of experience, ballast, a network of potential clients, and possibly, capital. And the younger partner can deliver the oomph factor – the get-up-and-go, the tech savvy, the ambition of someone in the early stages of his or her career, and an eagerness to try new ways of doing things.

Together, this kind of partnership creates a balanced business with legs that can be slowly built over time, with a long-term horizon.

In the following three chapters, you will meet entrepreneurial intergenerational teams who are pairing up for success.

CHAPTER 9

Ginning Things Up

Michael Lowe (r) and John Uselton (l),
New Columbia Distillers

Michael Lowe was weary of retirement.

He had exited the workforce in 2008, following a 30-year legal career, the lion's share of it spent as a corporate lawyer for Verizon. He was taking yoga classes five days a week and reading like a fiend. In retirement, the snag was that his wife, Melissa Kroning, registrar of the Smithsonian American Art Museum, was still working full time.

"I was just kind of hanging around the house," Lowe, now 69, said. "I decided I might as well try something else."

As luck would have it, he had a good relationship with his son-in-law, John Uselton, now 45, then a beer buyer for a liquor store and a waiter, and a fellow aficionado of home brewing, wine collecting, and spirits. The two men had built a solid rapport since Lowe's daughter,

Elizabeth, began dating Uselton a decade earlier. So they began to literally gin up some ideas about possible projects they might collaborate on. On a lark, Lowe enrolled in a weekend distilling class at Cornell University, and realized making spirits was something they could do together if Uselton was game.

After getting his son-in-law on board, the two headed to Dry Fly Distilling in Spokane, Washington, for an apprenticeship to get their hands dirty and learn to operate the equipment. They were hooked.

When they returned, they began cooking up a distinctive artisanal recipe for gin – a spirit they both savored. Their winning blend combined 100% wheat grain needed for the brew (soft red winter wheat, specifically, from the Northern Neck of Virginia) with juniper (the primary botanical used in gin), lemon and grapefruit peel, sage, cinnamon, coriander, and celery seed.

Their shared passion for craft distilling ultimately grew into New Columbia Distillers (greenhatgin.com), the first microdistillery in Washington, D.C. In 2012, it rolled out the first bottling of its smallbatch Green Hat distilled gin from a nearly century-old warehouse holding their 15-foot solid copper still. It was named for George Cassiday, a famous Capitol Hill bootlegger from the 1920s, who donned a green felt fedora on his hooch-selling forays into Congress.

Start-ups like Lowe and Uselton's are a new curve in the rising senior entrepreneurship trend, and a variation of traditional family businesses: so-called legacy partnerships. The partnerships are begun soon after the older partner's retirement from a decades-long career, and the early stages of the next generation down's career liftoff. The two generations bring balancing assets to a young business. The assets are normally capital and experience from the senior partner and vim, vigor, technical capability, and digital marketing savvy from the younger.

The most important thing is having a sharp idea of what each partner brings to the venture. "We use a lot of what we learned in our backgrounds," Uselton says.

He and Lowe share operating the still and creating recipes. Having worked as a beer buyer for a liquor store and a waiter at a popular Dupont Circle restaurant, Obelisk, before dropping into the distilling business, Uselton had an expansive network of contacts in the restaurant and beverage business in the region. And his outgoing nature paid off at tastings given at local businesses, which were crucial in driving interest in the pair's artisanal gin.

Lowe is in charge of finances and compliance issues. He was a regulatory lawyer in his former life at Verizon. The partners had to get legislation passed through the District of Columbia City Council to be licensed to sell the gin at the distillery and host tastings.

The real appeal for this two-generation team? "You get to make something. You get to be hands on. There is a lot of stuff you get to do, and, at the end of the day, you have something to show for what you've done," Uselton says.

Communication counts. "If something isn't right, we talk about it, we raise it, we resolve it," Lowe says. "We don't let it accumulate. Whether we're related or not, in this small environment, working hand in glove there will be tiny issues. Being family gives us even more incentive to make sure we don't let something potentially fester. We're both very conscious of that."

One thing that equalizes their responsibilities: "I am a skinny little old guy. I can't do a lot of the physical stuff," Lowe says. "John can lift the big hoses, cases, and bags of grain. There's a lot of physical labor involved."

With both men working 50-hour weeks, in 2018 the distillery is on track to produce 5,000 cases of gin (retail price: $36 a fifth) for sale to 80 liquor stores and 200 bars and restaurants in Washington, and a growing number of outlets in Delaware, Maryland, and Virginia. Lowe figures that he has financed close to $1 million of his and his wife's savings in the business. But, he says, with $900,000 in revenue projected for 2018, he has been repaying it and the business is profitable.

Lowe says that both men came up with the idea of the distillery. "It seemed like it might give John a leg up, but it was up to him to decide voluntarily if he thought it was a good move," he said. "It was a fair amount of risk for him to give up his day job and put all of his energy into this. It's nice to think that I will probably do this for 8 or 10 years, but it should be able to continue, and John can carry on."

Making It Work

I asked Michael and John to look back and share their thoughts on starting an intergenerational business.

Kerry: What did starting your own business mean to you personally?

For both of us, applying our creativity to make a number of products that people like has been the most important aspect of this business.

Were you confident that you were doing the right thing? Any second-guessing?

Michael: When we started, we were not at all sure the business would work. When we were still in business after our first year, we were very gratified that we had found and filled a niche that allowed us to build a viable business.

Anything you would have done differently?

Michael: We probably should have started with more capital. Each new equipment purchase and hiring decision was a tough decision because we did not have the resources to make them routine.

How do you measure your success?

Michael: We measure it primarily by our penetration into the market with a variety of products that our customers want.

How big a role did financial rewards play in your decision?

Michael: It was more of an issue for John, who gave up a full-time position to take this risk in the hope of building a successful business. For me, additional financial reward was not the main motivator, although I was hoping to recoup my investment while exercising my creativity and building a family business.

How did your preparation help you succeed?

John: My background in the retail alcohol and restaurant business in D.C. was essential in understanding and communicating to our market. Michael's background eased our navigating the regulatory and legislative minefields of starting a highly regulated business.

What do you tell other people who ask for your advice?

Michael: Make sure you have a market opening ahead of you. We were fortunate that, as the first D.C. distillery, our market was open. As more distilleries have entered the market, it has gotten tougher for new start-ups to distinguish themselves. Second, make sure you have and stick to a distinctive vision for your products. Novelty can sell the first bottle, but quality and distinctiveness are essential to sell the customer a second one.

What are some of the unexpected rewards and surprises?

John: The biggest reward is in developing a new product from concept, through multiple recipes, to a production process, and then favorable reaction from our customers.

What was the biggest challenge?

Michael: Running a small business, especially a heavily regulated one, requires continuous juggling of a range of bookkeeping, compliance, personnel and customer- and vendor-relations tasks – usually on deadline. You can't let these tasks obscure the reasons you got started with the business.

WHAT'S BEHIND THE MOVEMENT

"Many seniors are creating legacy businesses alongside a younger member of their family," Elizabeth Isele, founder of the Global Institute for Experienced Entrepreneurship, told me. "It's a winning formula for both generations."

While data documenting these new generational pairings is anecdotal, the trend appears to be gathering momentum in today's economy. The unemployment rate among older Americans is lower than for younger Americans,

(Continued)

WHAT'S BEHIND THE MOVEMENT (*Cont'd*)

but government statistics show that once older Americans lose their jobs, they tend to be unemployed for far longer, as finding new work is much more difficult. And full-time work is elusive for many younger workers, with a large segment of millennials working contract and part-time positions and cobbling together a series of side gigs to make ends meet. Given those realities, one can definitely see how those two demographics might team up as entrepreneurs.

Multigenerational start-ups are leading the way in particular demographic groups, Isele says. For example, Hispanic entrepreneurs are known for creating legacy businesses. Family members working together often create small retail establishments like florist shops, restaurants and other businesses in the food industry, and service businesses like cleaning companies.

The culture has a lot to do with that movement to join up to work together. Hispanic culture emphasizes taking care of elders and a deep-seated obligation to care for one another. Starting a multigenerational business flows from that inner respect and support for one another.

Another communal benefit for senior and junior entrepreneurs can be a moral purpose, Isele says. "People at this age really want to create a business that has some kind of social impact on their community, if not the world. And often the younger workers carry the same sense of idealism on their sleeves."

6 STEPS TO A POSITIVE SENIOR-JUNIOR PAIRING

- **Practice patience.** Take the time to teach your younger partner the ropes – even things as simple as how to dress properly for client meetings. Things that may seem natural to you may not be obvious to someone newly arrived in the working world.
- **Open the lines of communication.** As with any partnership, communication is the key. You must have regular daily meetings with transparency. Honesty is the core to a good partnership.
- **Divvy up chores.** You can't micromanage. Delegating tasks makes this a true partnership, so create a clear division of responsibilities that will tap into both partners' strengths.
- **Ramp up education.** Look for career-building education opportunities for your junior partner, so they can keep moving ahead and advancing their skill set. You should also stay afoot of trends in your industry and beyond, so don't neglect your own lifelong learning.
- **Manage client relationships.** You may need to play the grownup in the partnership with customers who aren't hip to the dynamic duo. Be clear

with your partner when and if this is necessary if someone is reluctant to deal exclusively with your younger cofounder. He or she will quickly show they are up for the job, but it can take some hand holding.
- **Be a mentor and a mentee.** Yes, this is a partnership, but you can't avoid taking on the role of mentor, and you shouldn't. You should be available to teach and transfer your knowledge to your younger partner. In reverse, you should be open to mentoring help from him or her as well.

How to Run a Family Business Successfully

Rob Lachenauer, a partner and CEO at Banyan Global Family Business Advisors in Boston, says there's one thing that makes family businesses different from all others. "In a non-family business, you can quit your job and it's usually a career enhancing move. In a family business, you sure can't quit your family," Lachenauer told me.

As someone who grew up working for my family's business during high school and college, I know what he means. If you're in a family business or thinking about starting one, you'll want to see the following highlights from the advice Lachenauer offered when I interviewed him.

I also suggest you check out the new website Familybusiness.org, an offshoot of the Entrepreneur and Innovation Exchange (eix. org), a social media platform aimed at improving the success rate of new business ventures. (Full disclosure: The Schulze Foundation, which funds EIX, is also a funder of Next Avenue.)

> *Kerry: What are the biggest challenges family businesses face that other businesses don't, and how can families best deal with them?*

Rob Lachenauer: One is the complexity of the relationships they are dealing with, and two is that owners are people in a family business. Not institutions.

Sometimes you're really dealing with emotional events that happened way, way back when. Every decision in a family business has lifelong implications to relationships in the family. That is one of the biggest things that's different. Try firing your niece and then inviting her to your Thanksgiving dinner.

Add to that that everyone is playing multiple roles. In a nonfamily business, your boss is your boss. Sometimes you love him, sometimes you hate him. In a family business, your boss can be your dad, a brother. I liken it to a house of mirrors. You see everyone five times at once. You see several versions of people looking at you. Who am I talking to? Who is listening right now? Are you the CEO, dad, mentor? When you add the confusion of roles to the lifelong relationship, it is fraught with peril.

The other thing that is so different is that owners are people. In family businesses, you will act in a way that others see as "irrational," meaning not necessarily for profit-maximizing at every step.

They may be saying, 'What is a greater joy than to come to a business I love and working day-to-day with my son?' Is his son a rock star? No. He's pretty good, but if he was looking after profits, he would hire someone else rather than his son.

What makes some family businesses succeed while others fail?

Managing the family part of the family business is the key. People who are great at this work diligently on keeping the family unified. They communicate a lot. They have experiences – family assemblies once a year, for example. They have fun, and they talk about what the purpose of their family is, why they stay united.

Others can fail, for example, if they don't manage generational transition. It is a vulnerable time when the older generation doesn't want to get off the playing field. They will delay their own retirement and discussions about bringing in the next generation too long, and if you wait too long you can't do it.

What's your advice for working with your children in the business?

The two most valued assets that an owner of a family business will have are: one, her children, and two, her business. But when these two things come together, they can become paralyzed in doubt and bad decision making.

We have seen family businesses overpromote and overpay family members. It's nepotism at its worst. We have also seen them do the opposite – underpromote and underpay. "It should be an honor to work here, we are going to pay you less."

Your instincts are a little off when a child is involved. The advice is they should have a family employment policy. You make it a policy, not personal. You can't treat Jack better than Jill. You have to be clear on how to attract the next generation, entice them into the business, and recruit them. How do you hire them? Do they come in on their merit, or do they get a special something?

And you have to be clear on how you develop family members. Do they have an escalator to the top, or do they have to work their way up? How do you evaluate them? Often, they are soft-balled and not developed properly and given clear feedback. How do you compensate them? Is it merit based, or market based?

Importantly, what are the exit rules? Can you fire a family member? Our experience is they exit from the business and they exit from the family. They are so ashamed. Their whole identity has been taken away from them.

Other advice: Don't have your children report directly to you. And always have them work outside the family business before coming in. They need to learn the real world.

What's your advice for working with your siblings in the business?

The best relationships are the ones who are very good at syncing up. So, for example, every morning they will have an hour sync-up and talk about business, what's going on, then say, "OK, let's go." They very actively make sure they overcommunicate with each other to make sure any misgivings can't get in the way of family business.

What's your advice for working with your older parents in the business?

This is probably the hardest one. I would say the majority of family business founders are monarchs, and they never want to leave. Don't expect them to change.

They believe they are the reason the business exists, and they often are. All power to them. They want to be in the chair, not playing golf, or on a charity board. That's their life. It's their place to go. It's a delicate dance.

In what way is starting and running a family business harder these days than in the past?

Attracting family members to your business is getting harder. Why I say that is, where do college graduates in business want to work these days? Google, Facebook, Apple! They want sexy, tech businesses. Do I really want to return to Des Moines to run our corn-processing factory? Entering the family business can be a one-way street with no exit plan. If you exit, you are exiting the business and often the family.

You need to have a really connected family to have a successful family business. Today, family members are more mobile and global. Realistically, it is harder to stay together and connected and they need to do it in person, so they really have that connection. How do you do that when everyone is everywhere around the world? That is just a logistical issue that our families face a lot.

Chapter Recap

In this chapter, we learned how two generations can build an entity together that can last not just a few years but for decades. The factors that work to build any partnership come into play, but the idea of an intergenerational partnership provides an opportunity to combine the best qualities of each age with the experience and knowledge they each bring to the business.

YOUR TO-DO LIST

- In your journal, write down the best qualities and skills you and your younger partner possess. How will they complement each other?
- What will your working relationship look like? Write down your vision.
- Take time to explore how you will feel working side by side on a daily basis with someone decades younger than you, from whom you might have to take direction.

CHAPTER 10

The Whole Million-Dollar Package

Paul Tasner, PulpWorks

Paul Tasner was at loose ends. After a 40-plus-year career handling supply chains at corporations like Clorox and California Closets, during a downsizing, he lost the San Francisco–based strategic management post he had held for three years at Method Products, which makes environmentally friendly soaps and household cleaners.

That was 2009, and he was then 64.

"Retirement, like for so many people, was not an option for me," he says in his TED Talk titled "How I Became an Entrepreneur at 66," which has over two million views. "So I turned to consulting for the next couple of years without any passion whatsoever."

Tasner worried that he might never land another top full-time job. So he devised an idea for a potential new business, motivated somewhat by his time at Method, where he had experienced a late-in-life switch to a deep concern for preserving the earth. As Tasner told me, "I felt a passion to make a difference for people and the planet."

His other incentive was struggling while trying to open a package of kitchen shears his wife had recently bought. We can all relate to the frustration Tasner felt as he struggled to tear open that hard plastic package. "Ridiculous," he says.

An engineer by training, Tasner set off on a mission to gather all the data he could about how to make a package that was simpler to open. And with his newly founded sensibility, he wanted to learn as much as possible about packaging that would be recycled and biodegradable.

While molding recycled goods into packaging isn't novel – egg cartons are a familiar example – Tasner knew that most sellers wouldn't want to show their goods in something so dowdy. His exploration led him to processes and materials that could be combined to turn paper, cardboard, and sugarcane fiber into a thin but sturdy, glossy-white packaging material.

Hoping to construct a green manufacturing facility, he started another hunt – this time on LinkedIn, where he connected with Elena Olivari, a local architect dedicated to sustainability, who was two decades his junior. "I was looking for a new job that would give me a stronger feeling of purpose," she says. "When Paul briefly explained why he was writing to me, my wishes were answered."

For Tasner, it was a calling. "I wanted to build my own business … replacing the toxic disposable plastic packaging to which we've all become addicted," he says. "This is called clean technology … so now at the age of 66, with 40 years of experience, I became an entrepreneur for the very first time."

And the future was in his favor. Tasner cites data from the Chartered Management Institute that shows older entrepreneurs have a 70% success rate for launching new ventures, versus 28% for their younger counterparts.

Teaming up to form PulpWorks (pulpworksinc.com), they spent $25,000 to design and build a prototype package – a smooth and colorful alternative to plastic – then applied for and received a patent on the product they dubbed Karta-Pack.

Tasner and Olivari spent nearly all of 2012 pitching venture capitalists to raise the $17 million they calculated they would need to build a factory. They got nowhere. Tasner never imagined that investors wouldn't want to do well by doing good. "You're never too old to be naive," he jokes.

"I can't tell you how demoralizing it was to look for investors – it was downright humiliating. We were dismissed in favor of younger entrepreneurs, and the investment community wasn't excited about creating packages out of waste," Tasner says.

"It can be very intimidating and discouraging," he adds. "I have shoes older than most of these people. I had no role models. The 20-something app developer from Silicon Valley was no role model."

Their thrifty ways – and backing from their families – helped the duo carry on. (Tasner says his wife, a registered nurse with her own healthcare start-up, "never blinked an eye about supporting PulpWorks.") Each partner had invested $50,000 in nonretirement savings at the get-go, financing the funds "in slow drips" to develop prototypes, apply for a patent, and travel to trade shows and meetings with possible investors. They worked then (and still do) in home offices and shared office spaces like WeWork, meeting once or twice a week. Once it sunk in that they wouldn't get their $17 million, they modified their business plan to one requiring little upfront cash. Instead of building a plant, they'd outsource production, licensing the design to other makers.

The fresh tactic worked, helping PulpWorks open for business with its first sale in March of 2014 and land contracts with companies including Google, Energizer, and Anthropologie. A big benefit was the professional network Tasner had developed over decades in the industry. "We don't always have the perfect person to sit down with," he says, "but we always have someone who can at least open the door to us and point us in the right direction."

Revenue is expected to hit $1 million in 2018, and the business carries no debt. Tasner and Olivari now each take salaries of about $60,000 a year, and the business is profitable.

"I've spent almost my entire life doing exactly what we're doing here with PulpWorks," Tasner says. "But I've done it for employers, not for myself. It's an amazing feeling."

Even better, "I am doing the most rewarding and meaningful work of my life right now," he says in his TED Talk.

Making It Work

I asked Paul to look back and share his thoughts on starting a packaging business when he was over 60.

Kerry: *What did starting your own business mean to you personally?*

Paul: It was the realization of a life-long interest, perhaps, even passion at times. I never felt completely comfortable in the corporate world.

Were you confident that you were doing the right thing? Any second-guessing?

Actually, and surprisingly, I was always confident that this business was the right thing at the right time for me.

Anything you would have done differently?

Many things. We began with five cofounders. We really didn't need all five cofounders. Three of our start-up team could very easily have been advisers or consultants in retrospect. We looked for funding for far too long. We should have seen the handwriting on the wall much sooner.

How do you measure your success?

By the way I feel. I have never been this pleased and proud of my work. How can that not be interpreted as "successful"!

How big a role did financial rewards play in your decision?

A modest role. Yes, financial rewards were important but not to the exclusion of all else.

How did your preparation help you succeed?

Because our business is not a great leap from the work that I did as an employee, one might say that I had 40 years of preparation. All of my work leading up to the founding of PulpWorks has been an incredibly valuable resource and foundation.

What do you tell other people who ask for your advice?

I tell them to find a good partner to share the joy and pain. Also, I suggest that they enter new business competitions to gain free exposure and potential financial rewards.

What books did you find helpful?

Candidly, I couldn't bear to read about business in the too few hours that I spend away from my work. So, my reading is almost entirely that of fiction. It provides a wonderful mental break from the business.

What are some of the unexpected rewards and surprises?

I'm told that I've been an inspiration to some. Especially after my TED Talk was posted. That is a role that I never envisioned for myself. It's an honor, a privilege, a gift. Truly, it is.

What was the biggest challenge?

Sales. I'm not a natural salesperson. Being successful at sales is very difficult. I have a whole new admiration for good salespeople. It's an art – and a science.

ADVICE FOR SELLING YOUR START-UP IDEA TO INVESTORS

Perfect your pitch. To sell your idea, you must be bold and brazen and have some razzle-dazzle, but do it in a couple of sentences. Make sure one of those says how your customer will use it.

Prepare an honest market analysis. What's your niche? Why is there room for one more operator? You will be asked.

Know your numbers. An investor wants to make sure you are as sharp about the financials as you are about your sales pitch. If you aren't the one to do this, make sure you have someone on your team who can lend the expertise when you're in the hot seat. For instance, an investor clearly wants to get a sense of when your business might be able to operate in the black.

Assemble your personal board of advisers. Pick three or four pros to help you smooth your pitch and serve as your sherpas to possible investors and also customers. Search your network of business contacts to see who might have the expertise and the time to provide some unbiased help. These can be virtual meetings.

ARE THESE THE BEST CITIES FOR BOOMER ENTREPRENEURS?

There's something compelling about a "Best Places" list that's tough to resist. And as someone who often writes about entrepreneurship, I was doubly intrigued by the LendingTree ranking: The Best Cities for Baby Boomer Entrepreneurs, which compared the 50 biggest U.S. metropolitan statistical areas.

I must admit, though, the findings were a little surprising to me, since I wouldn't have considered some of them hotbeds for boomer business launches. I'll tell you which places scored best momentarily, but here's a hint: after learning about them, you may find yourself humming "California Dreamin'" by The Mamas & The Papas.

LendingTree's Latest List of Places for Entrepreneurs

This list was the latest in a series of entrepreneurship location lists from LendingTree, following The Places with the Youngest Entrepreneurs and Best Places for Women Entrepreneurs.

The idea of looking for the best cities for boomer start-ups is especially timely, since this is clearly a demographic increasingly hankering to be their own boss. The Kaufmann Foundation has regularly noted this group being more likely than 20-somethings in starting new businesses, and female entrepreneurs over 50 have particularly been on the rise.

No. 1: San Jose

LendingTree calls San Jose – the Silicon Valley hub – the best place for boomer entrepreneurs. "In addition to representing high business income, San Jose boasts the largest share of boomer business founders," according to Kali McFadden, senior research and analyst at LendingTree.

But McFadden told me that she, too, was surprised San Jose came in first. "When you think of San Jose, you think of start-up tech and a young-man's-game kind of thing," she noted.

According to LendingTree, the average business income among baby boomer entrepreneurs in San Jose is $47,401, the highest among all 50 cities examined. And the boomer entrepreneurs' annual median business income is $13,602, ranking fifth. In the last five years, more than one in four of San Jose's new businesses was run by a boomer, the highest percentage among all cities surveyed.

Other Cities Called Best for Boomer Entrepreneurs

San Francisco ranked second. (It also came in first on LendingTree's Best Places for Women Entrepreneurs.) The city by the bay has the highest annual median income for business owners who are boomers: $16,827. It was No. 2 for average business income, at $45,505 a year. San Francisco also has a large share of entrepreneurial boomers, with one in every five new business founders born between 1946 and 1964.

Boston earned third place. "Boomer Bostonians have a median business income of $14,106, one of the highest figures for boomer entrepreneurs across the country," according to the researchers. It also has the second-highest rate of new businesses founded by boomers – 20.3% – tied with Memphis.

Sacramento, California's capital, was No. 4 and placed second for median earnings among self-employed boomers: $15,114. The average business income boomers earn is also on the upper end, at $37,314.

And No. 5 is Nashville, which also ranks fifth for the percentage of new businesses opened by boomers: 19.1%. Nashville shares second place with Sacramento for the median business earnings for boomers.

Rounding out the Top 10: Hartford, Connecticut; Houston; Austin, Texas; Los Angeles; and Memphis.

The Ranking's Worst Big Cities for Boomer Entrepreneurs

The bottom dwellers: New Orleans, Miami, and Orlando.

Boomers in New Orleans – No. 50 out of 50 – earn a median business income of just $1,008, less than 13% of the national average. Yikes. And boomer entrepreneurs there take home $20,562 each year on average, which is only two-thirds of the national average.

Even worse, according to LendingTree, in Orlando (and Tampa), self-employed boomers earn a median business income of $0.

I find it hard to imagine an expensive city like San Francisco being a great place to launch a business. Wouldn't you think the basic costs of bricks and mortar and hiring employees would hamper financial success, at least in the early days?

The LendingTree Methodology

Here's how LendingTree came up with its ranking: Each metro area was scored on median business income for boomers, average (mean) business income for boomers, and the percentage of businesses founded in the last five years started by boomers. All three factors were weighted evenly.

"Medians can tell us how much most people are earning, while the average can give us a sense of how much income there is overall," according to McFadden. "A bigger gap between median and average indicates that there is a lot of money to be made, but fewer people are earning it."

To determine the percentage of new businesses founded by boomers, LendingTree looked at those seeking loans on their business loan platform. "This is a clue about how attractive and hospitable metros are to entrepreneurs in that age bracket," said McFadden.

She concedes that "expensive cities do seem to favor boomers." Her explanation: "It's likely that there are a higher number of professionals winding down their careers in those cities and may be hanging out that shingle to start consulting and may not have too much in overhead costs."

Boomers in these cities, McFadden added, may also have money saved and the network and the contacts to go solo there. Moreover, expensive places may translate to cities where you can charge more for your services, hence high reported earnings.

Concerns About the Numbers

But the numbers are still problematic to me. There is a pretty large difference between median and average incomes reported. Then, too, the data doesn't drill down to what kinds of businesses the boomers are starting and if they are part time or full-blown, seven-days-a-week, all-pistons-rolling start-ups.

"It's unfortunate that we can't get more detail in the data," said McFadden. "I am a number cruncher, and it is frustrating."

How to Choose a Place to Start a Business

My bottom line: The best way to decide where to start your business is pretty basic, and the location doesn't need to be a best place at all. Ask yourself: Do you have a market for the goods or services you want to sell? Is there a labor supply available if you'll need to hire workers? What kind of licensing and other bureaucratic hurdles might the state or municipality have where you want to launch?

Before opening shop, it's critical to research local regulations ranging from business licensing laws to small-business tax incentives. You should also scrutinize other new ventures in the city to see which are successful.

And for advice, there are SCORE programs (retired business professionals offering free tips to start-up founders) in every major city.

A parting thought from McFadden: "Depending on where you live, quite possibly getting a part-time job might be more economically sensible for people than starting a business." As The Mamas & The Papas liked to sing, dream a little dream ...

Chapter Recap

In this chapter, we learned the importance of blending skill sets with a younger cofounder, the frustrations of trying to raise capital in a world of youthful entrepreneurs, and the importance of being nimble and open to revising your plans as you move forward.

YOUR TO-DO LIST

- Write down in your journal what skills you need from a partner to make your business a reality.
- Consider carefully where your funding is likely to come from.
- Reflect on what city you want to launch your business in, if you have the choice of relocating.

CHAPTER 11

Cookie Contessas

Bergen Giordani (r) & Morgen Giordani
Reamer (l), One Hot Cookie

This picture is credited to ICON of Youngstown.

For Bergen Giordani and her daughter, Morgen Giordani Reamer, starting a business together has been sweet in more ways than one.

In 2013, when they launched their retail dessert shop, One Hot Cookie (onehotcookie.com), in their hometown of Youngstown, Ohio, it was a win-win. "The idea for the business came from our desire to do something together," says Bergen, president of the company and a single mom. "We both love hot, gooey desserts and sweets, and since Morgen, now vice president of the operation, was a child, we would go out and get a dessert somewhere and have that special time together."

Moreover, it was an opportunity for Bergen to find work she loved and a chance to combine that with baking cookies alongside her then-teenage daughter, an activity they had relished doing together since Morgen was tiny.

While waiting to see if the business would gain traction and become profitable, Bergen worked full time until recently outside the business as development director at the Rich Center for Autism, located on the campus of Youngstown State University, where she led a half-million-dollar-a-year campaign to support children affected by autism. And initially she worked part time as a bartender, as well. "I wanted to make sure Morgen, who was 16 when we started, and I were provided for. And I attribute a lot of our ability to grow to that work ethic of working really hard on our business while I was still working outside of the business," Bergen says.

Morgen didn't neglect her education. She graduated in 2018 with a BS in medical laboratory science from Youngstown State University. Ohio has a program where you can "double down" your senior year in high school, so during her senior year in high school she was a freshman in college. She did, however, take some time off from running the business for her senior year of college, because her program required her to study and work at the Cleveland Clinic, so she moved to Cleveland from June 2017 to May 2018.

The mother-daughter relationship did take some effort as well. For Morgen, working together has had its benefits, but also its challenges. "On one hand, she [Bergen] understands everything in my life, because she is my mom, my best friend, my business partner," Morgen says. "That's great most of the time, but at first it was rocky. We had a hard time dialing into what role we were when. When we are home, we shouldn't talk about work, but concentrate on what we are doing like a mother and daughter, not business partners."

Bergen, too, struggled with how to navigate their new relationship. " We realized that compartmentalizing it didn't work. The roles were blurred. Whenever I have a freakout at her at work, people would be looking at us."

"I'd say, it's okay, she's my mom," Morgen recalled. "I'm not going to get fired. She's being my mom right now."

In reality, the partners, who are two decades apart, balance each other well. "She is tougher than I am," Morgen says. "I help bring her down a little, but she brings me up at little, so we meet in the middle. I have also grown into being a boss and a leader in the last couple of years, and she has taught me how to do that. It was hard for me to tell someone what to do, who might be 30, but I'm not 16 anymore."

More specifically, the two women bring different skills to their venture, which now has stores in Ohio and Pennsylvania. "Morgen is really into the details and the organizational part of things," Bergen says. "She can pick up details and things taking place in one store and not another and steer the operational ship. I do more of the larger-picture, long-term planning five years down the road. Morgen is working on what's happening now."

Their start-up was, however, by the seat of their pants. "We started with about $2,500 in cash and all of the zebra-print furniture from Morgen's bedroom that we put in our first storefront in Youngstown's Erie Terminal Building," Bergen says. "I was broke. I really didn't have any money. This idea came to me that we should try this, everyone loved our cookies, and the pieces started to fall into place. It was almost like when you have so little you have nothing to lose. I thought, 'You know, what is $2,500? It's not going to change our lives one way or the other.' But I was wrong. It certainly changed our lives. That capital went to the initial equipment purchase and our first month's rent."

Today, One Hot Cookie sells traditional cookies like chocolate chip, oatmeal, peanut butter, snickerdoodle, and sugar, and is celebrated for specialty cookies that are covered with frosting and tasty toppings. The company currently has 30 employees, online ordering nationwide, and one franchisee. Meantime, Morgen is exploring a new doughnut-centered concept, Oh! Donuts. For that venture, in a shift of roles, Morgen assumes the role of president and Bergen, vice-president. "We are hopeful that we can open that concept by Q2 2019," says Bergen.

To expand their reach, franchising will be a big part of the strategy for 2019, Bergen says. "We kind of fell into franchising. Our franchisee found us; we were very honest, and told her, 'Hey, we are set up for it legally, but I'm not sure we're ready.' So as long as she knew it was going to be a learning curve, we were on board."

For Robin Barnby, that franchisee, who had spent more than three decades working as a registered nurse and vice president for a retail pharmacy, all it took was a visit to one of the retail stores and she was hooked. In the fall of 2017, she contacted Bergen to see whether franchising was an option. Barnby had been on what she called a sabbatical trying to figure out what her next act was going to be. She had offers in the medical field but was itching to do something different.

"We were very candid to start this relationship off," Bergen says. "We are all in this together. We both look at each other as partners in each other's success." Barnby has one store in Berlin, Ohio, but she plans to open other One Hot Cookie shops in Akron, Cleveland, Canton, and perhaps the Columbus area.

The move into franchising has, however, required a shift in how the mother and daughter approach things with their business operations. "We have to plan a little ahead and be proactive," Bergen says. "We need to make sure Barnby has the information, all the necessary paperwork and marketing materials and ingredients. It's not just us anymore, and doing things a little further in advance is challenging."

The beauty is still in the simplicity of the concept. "We are just baking cookies and brownies and serving them with ice cream," Morgen says. "When you walk into one of our stores, everything is pink and black and modern, and there are pictures of our adorably cute dogs – a pug, Kate Middleton, and a yellow lab, Remington."

The dogs, in fact, are a big part of their family-friendly atmosphere. "Our dogs are always with us," Morgen says. "We're open until 2:30 a.m. on weekends in our Youngstown store, and you can't leave your dogs at home." The duo also sells a line of all natural dog cookies. (Full disclosure: My Lab, Zena, is a huge fan and stares longingly at the box on the counter.)

"We want to make it a fun experience for our customers," Bergen says. "We know that cookies are a commodity. When you come to One Hot Cookie, it needs to be something more."

To spread the word, the pair has relied on social media as a way of connecting to cookie enthusiasts on Instagram and Facebook. The women regularly post snaps of their cookies and comical photos of their dogs. "Starting a new business with no advertising, marketing, or promotional budget meant that we had to really tap into social media hard," Bergen says. "To get that grassroots growth, you have to be clever and truly be authentic."

Making It Work

I asked Bergen and Morgen to look back and share their thoughts on starting a mother-daughter cookie business.

Kerry: What did starting your own business mean to you personally?

Bergen: Starting the business was really fulfilling personally. When you create something from nothing, it's like your baby. There was definitely a sense of accomplishment there. The first year it was just fun to see what it was doing and how it was going, and then it became a real business. And we realized we had a viable business model on our hands here, and it was really incredible.

Morgen: Now it means the world to me. I couldn't imagine my life without One Hot Cookie. We didn't know what we were getting ourselves into, and it was, "Hey we're rolling with this." I did have to take some time to realize that One Hot Cookie was not something I had to do, or was something I was forced into, but this is something I wanted to do.

Were you confident that you were doing the right thing? Any second-guessing?

Bergen: "Ever forward" is my motto. I admit, I do second-guess at times. Any time in a small business when there is a hiccup and something doesn't go your way, you think, why am I putting myself through this? Then I ask: Why wouldn't we? This is now something that is bigger than the two of us.

Anything you would have done differently?

Bergen: I would have been more strategic in our growth. Once we had the opportunity to grow, we kind of went with it. Maybe being a little more patient and waiting for the right opportunity would have helped. (The pair have had to shutter two stores.)

How do you measure your success?

Morgen: The best way to measure our success is sales growth. The flow of customers throughout the day and how much money the business is bringing in. Also it's wonderful when around the community, you hear random people talking about One Hot Cookie. Who would have thought five years ago that this idea would become something that other families are enjoying?

Bergen: Same-store sales are in the six figures and have been climbing double-digits year over year. We can pay ourselves salaries. And we're growing. In 2019, we will have three stores that are ours – two in Ohio and one in Wexford, Pennsylvania, plus one that is franchised in Berlin, Ohio.

How big a role did financial rewards play in your decision?

Bergen: In the short term, we were not looking for immediate financial rewards. I was working outside the business. But we had a great idea, some good cookies, and have put in some hard work, and the rewards are starting to come in.

How did your preparation help you succeed?

Bergen: We had shared cookies with friends and family and gone through that channel to get feedback. While the cookies are delicious, we really wanted it to be about people coming into the store and experiencing it. The first 18 months were about getting people to come in, and find out who we are and what makes our cookies different.

I took an executive-MBA-type program offered by the Small Business Administration – the SBA Emerging Leaders Initiative (sba.gov/about-sba/sba-initiatives/sba-emerging-leaders-initiative). You spend 15 weeks, one night a week, going to class and working in a cohort to develop your three-to-five-year business plan and more. (The SBA [sba.gov/learning-center] also offers a variety of online programs to help you start and run your business.)

Morgan: We didn't start marketing through community outreach, doing fairs and events, until we had been open a year. Serving hot cookies is difficult to replicate at events. And since we had no money for marketing, for fun we would dress our dog up in costumes and take pictures of him and put on Pinterest and social media. He became the unofficial mascot.

What do you tell other people who ask for your advice?

Bergen: You have to really love it. Whatever you are going to commit yourself to, you can't be there Monday to Friday. You are growing this thing and it is 100% a reflection of us in this small community, so you really have to be dedicated to it.

What books did you find helpful?

Bergen: One of the books that really helped me was *The E-Myth Revisited: Why Most Small Businesses Don't Work and What to Do About It* by Michael E. Gerber. It underscores the principle of working *on* your business, not just *in* your business. It makes you look at your business from a different angle. You have to go above it and ask what can I do to make it better in the long term? It's not stepping over dollars to pick up dimes. The second one is *Small Giants: Companies That Choose to Be Great Instead of Big* by Bo Burlingham. It's a great book about small businesses who are choosing to stay small and the great work they can do in their community.

What are some of the unexpected rewards and surprises?

Bergen: Being able to give back to the community and seeing the support from the community is so rewarding. We participate in fundraisers and charity events. It is marketing and outreach for us, but it's wonderful to support these organizations. It's important to us to do good for the community.

Morgen: Being in the store and seeing people here with their families. We do a lot of birthday parties in the store, and they are the biggest thing in the world when you are six years old!

What was the biggest challenge?

Bergen: It is very personal and it is very consuming.

IS FRANCHISING FOR YOU?

I had the opportunity to interview the stunningly successful founders of Panda Restaurant Group, the parent company of Panda Express, Panda Inn, and Hibachi-San, Andrew and Peggy Cherng. The Cherngs, now in their early 70s, spent the last 45 years building a Chinese restaurant empire that produced sales in excess of $3 billion last year, with over 2,000 Panda Express restaurants. Those restaurants each average about 480 guests daily, and the Cherngs employ more than 35,000 associates.

I know, this is not an example of a mid-life entrepreneurial couple, but the Cherngs' success is partly rooted in their decision *not* to franchise. They have regularly rejected chances to grow even quicker by franchising locations.

The beauty of not being franchised is you have control, restaurant industry analysts have told me. You have uniformity. When you have a franchise operation, even though guidelines are in place, all of the franchisees don't consistently play by the rule book.

While Bergen and Morgen are beginning to eye a growth path via franchising, and hopefully it will be a positive one for them, it can be a problematic path for both the franchisor and the franchisee.

That said, it seemed to me a good moment here to review some of the steps to take for those mid-life entrepreneurs like Robin Barnby, who like the idea of running their own business, but don't want the risk of starting from scratch. One way to do that certainly is to slide into entrepreneurship by purchasing a franchise.

About 10 years ago, Marvin Gay, now 76, a retired accountant, and his wife, Leslie, decided to open a Painting with a Twist franchise, in St. Petersburg, Florida. It was the first franchise location for Painting with a Twist, an art studio where groups of friends can gather to take a painting class together and sip beverages at the same time. The couple's start-up costs were nearly $40,000. To finance the business, they tapped their personal savings. A year and a half later, the Gays spent roughly $60,000 to open a second studio in Tampa. They subsequently sold that one and opened two more in Clearwater and Pinellas Park. They now operate three studios, all in Pinellas County. Last year, according to Marvin, the operations pulled in $800,000. After some growing pains, the studios are all in the black, drawing about 500+ paying customers weekly and allowing the Gays to draw salaries for themselves. The key to success in large measure has been their ability to self-finance.

The franchise route can be a good thing for budding entrepreneurs like the Gays. Many franchises offer a full range of services, including site selection, training, product supply, marketing plans, and even help in obtaining financing.

But it can be a complex and pricey road. An initial investment can range from $200,000 to $500,000. And it's not unusual to hear franchisees grumble about ongoing royalty and advertising fees. For example, Subway charges a standard $15,000 franchise fee (there are exceptions), and estimated start-up costs range from $89,550 to more than $300,000. Individual costs, however, vary by location, restaurant size, build-out costs, and more. On top of that, franchisees at Subway pay fees on a percentage of sales, royalties, and for advertising.

8 Tips to Help Avoid the Pitfalls:

1. **Do your research and soul-searching to determine if a franchise is really a good match for you.**

2. **Conduct a self-analysis.** I have found that those who are eager to get rolling often get caught up in the idea of the product or service but don't do the deep dive to determine if they really have the skills it takes to run it. What appeals to franchisors is someone who has a kit of business skills such as sales, marketing, leadership, communication, and customer service.

3. **Understand that you are not really the boss.** You must respect the blueprint. Franchises rely on the precise implementation of their business plan, not yours.

4. **Hire pros to help.** It's essential that you have a reputable franchise attorney and accountant to review the license agreement.

5. **Be a gumshoe.** The franchise industry is regulated by the Federal Trade Commission (ftc.gov), which provides an excellent consumer guide to buying a franchise and resources to help you avoid common scams. You will want to request a franchisor's disclosure document. It provides contact information for previous purchasers in your area, audited financial statements, a breakdown of start-up and ongoing costs, and an outline of your duties and the franchisor's responsibilities. It's important to get a sense of turnover of franchise units. Names and phone numbers of former and current franchisees in your area should be listed.

6. **Contact former franchisees to find out why they're no longer in business.** It might be, for instance, that the pledged training didn't occur for them, or the vigorous marketing backing that was plugged up front never happened. Talk to franchisees, preferably in person.

7. **Be realistic.** According to my reporting, about 20% of franchises knock it out of the park, 60% make a good living, and 20% are less successful. You want to get a feel for whether you have enough saved to really make a go of it. Operating costs on a monthly basis can be higher than you expect. Most franchisees I have talked to say it took them at least a year to begin to draw a salary.

(*Continued*)

IS FRANCHISING FOR YOU? (*Cont'd*)

8. **Look for the stamp of approval.** Find out if the franchise you're considering has the U.S. Small Business Administration's stamp of approval. This helps if you are seeking bank financing for a loan. SBA-approved franchises are ones whose disclosure agreements have been reviewed and accepted by the SBA. To find the list, go to sba.gov/document/support–sba-franchise-directory. The Franchise Registry at FRANdata.com is another good source for a range of information.

Check Out These Links:

- The U.S. Small Business Administration (sba.gov/course/introduction-franchising/) offers resources to help you get started.
- The American Association of Franchisees and Dealers (aafd.org) represents more than 50,000 franchised locations throughout the United States, representing more than 100 different franchise systems.
- The International Franchise Association (franchise.org) is a membership organization of franchisors, franchisees, and suppliers.
- Unhappy Franchisee (unhappyfranchisee.com) provides details of franchises gone sour.
- Blue MauMau (bluemaumau.org) has real accounts of the ins and outs of franchising.
- Franchise Direct (franchisedirect.com) provides financial specifics about a myriad of franchise operations.

Chapter Recap

In this chapter, we learned how a mother-and-daughter team are mixing up their own business with creativity and learning as they go. Their new foray into franchising is one way other mid-life entrepreneurs might choose to take the step into running their own business without all the preliminary legwork to test the idea. You gleaned various tips on how to explore this route.

YOUR TO-DO LIST

- Explore how you might use social media to ramp up your sales and court customers.
- Do you have a brand image that can serve as your mascot?
- Is owning a franchise appealing to you? If so, explore the links in the box to dig deep and see if it's the right choice for your entrepreneurial venture.

THE PATH TO SOCIAL ENTREPRENEURSHIP

There comes a time in our lives when we stop and pause and ask, is this what it's all about? Sometimes it is after the kids have launched, or we hit a milestone at work, or we lose someone we love too soon, too young.

It might even be a health crisis of our own that makes the fleeting passage of time all too real. There is a sensation, a longing that our time on this earth should have some lasting meaning or impact.

We have honed a skillset and a network and a confidence for getting things done, and it's time to do just that to make this a better world. Enter the social entrepreneur. Their start-up businesses are often nonprofits, but not always. Some for-profit businesses clearly can make a difference and provide a lasting legacy.

In the following four chapters, you will meet social entrepreneurs who have embarked on a variety of ventures to give back.

CHAPTER 12

Girl Power

Carol Nash, Bernadette's House

When Carol Nash retired seven years ago from Dimensions Healthcare System in Maryland after a long career in the nursing profession, she had no clue that she would soon be working harder than she ever did.

But Nash, now 74, is okay with that. "I burn with a passion for what I am doing," she says. "If I can make the difference in the life of one child, then I believe I have fulfilled a purpose here."

In 2012, Nash founded a small nonprofit, Bernadette's House (bernadetteshouse.org), based in Laurel, Maryland. The organization provides early intervention and prevention services through an afterschool mentoring program for girls 8 to 17 at risk of teenage pregnancy, drug addiction, or failing in school. "Helping people is what I've done my entire life," she says. "I guess I'm not really retiring."

Research from Encore.org, a nonprofit, shows that interest in starting a nonprofit between the ages of 50 and 70 has nearly doubled over the last three years, says Marc Freedman, founder of Encore.org and author of *How to Live Forever: The Enduring Power of Connecting the Generations.* "It's the combination of an upsurge in encore careers – second acts focused on the greater good – and the rise in boomers embracing entrepreneurship," he said.

There are those with a singular focus, like Nash, who are driven by personal life experience. She was raised from age 3 in the convent of the Franciscan Handmaids of Mary after the death of her mother. Her guardian there was Sister Maria Bernadette of the Franciscan Handmaids of Mary, an order of African American nuns. "I attribute my early development of self-esteem and confidence to her," Nash says.

Subsequently, as a registered nurse, Nash came into contact with "young women caught in an endless cycle of teen pregnancy and illiteracy." So when she retired, she realized she had a calling to support and develop young girls.

"I didn't know where the money was coming from, but I stepped out in faith, found a building close to home, started advertising, and kids started coming," she says.

Nash withdrew about $25,000 in retirement savings to set up the program. Donors helped provide furniture, fix a leaky roof, and paint the leased space. Volunteer mentors are professional women who make a one-year, one-hour-a-week minimum commitment to working with a child.

Each day after school, more than a dozen girls come to the white house, built in 1892, and stay until 6:30 p.m. There are a range of activities including learning etiquette, reading, dance classes, and more. There are "Girls Talk" sessions where the girls can have a heart-to-heart about anything on their mind, and they must also do simple chores such as washing dishes. The house has a kitchen, a dining room, a living room, an arts and crafts room, and a learning lab equipped with computers and a book-lined lounge.

Each girl is given a mentor, who shares new adventures with her, sometimes going to a ballet, a movie, or the theater, says Nash.

Bernadette's House also runs a summer program where girls can learn to play sports like lacrosse and tennis.

The organization operates mostly from donations and grants. "I believe these kids can really thrive if someone pays attention to them," Nash says. "I greet every girl each day with, 'Hello, beautiful' – and then give her a big hug."

Making It Work

I asked Carol to look back and share her thoughts on starting a nonprofit.

> **Kerry: What did starting your own nonprofit mean to you personally?**

Carol: A chance to fulfill what I felt was my God-ordained destiny, serving others through creating a safe place for girls to fulfill their dreams. The decision that I made was a declaration that I was following what God was calling me to do.

> **Were you confident that you were doing the right thing? Any second-guessing?**

There was no second-guessing! When I looked back over my unusual life, I felt I was created for this moment, and it was in line with what was needed in the world. As doors continued to open, I became more confident in this journey and that I was on the right path.

> **Anything you would have done differently?**

I would have planned better and had a stronger financial base to start. Also, I would have taken more time and used more wisdom when it came time to create the environment for the girls. Poor planning caused me to relocate several times.

> **How do you measure your success?**

I don't measure success in the typical fashion (by money), but by the number of people who come through the organization receiving the help they need. Not only the children, but the volunteers. I also measure success by the continuous resources that come through the door. That lets me know people really believe in the organization and understand the impact it has on the immediate community.

How did your preparation help you succeed?

Life experience and exposure helped prepare me to succeed. As a registered nurse, furthering my education in healthcare administration with an emphasis in organizational development and moving up my career path gave me the professional and interpersonal skills I needed to start an organization of my own.

Writing organizational procedures and developing policies during my career gave me an understanding of how to effectively communicate and execute a nonprofit business plan. It took over a year to do the legwork before I opened the doors of Bernadette's House. I also started small with just a handful of girls.

What do you tell other people who ask for your advice?

Don't be afraid to follow your dream, and never give up.

Take your time and think things through. Write it down and make it plain!

As you mature, so does your vision.

Choose kindness.

I always hope that people leave with a newfound sense of confidence after I've advised them.

You need to do your research, seek mentors, and make sure there's a genuine need for what it is you want to do. If you think you've found a niche and are fulfilling a need to make this a better place, then just do it; don't give up. Learn everything you can.

What books or resources did you use or recommend others to use?

Leap of Reason by Mario Morino, *The 48 Laws of Power* by Robert Greene, *A New Earth* by Eckhart Tolle, and *Visioneering* by Andy Stanley.

What are some of the unexpected rewards and surprises?

Finding my happy place at this age, while doing worthwhile work to support the dreams of others.

How easy it was for others to catch the vision.

Having my family and friends totally embrace my vision.

I'm always amazed at how things fall into place.

Lessons learned?

You're never too old to serve others; stay humble.

You must walk the talk for others; to believe in your vision.

Never give up; reaching your goal is just a matter of time.

When dealing with criticism, keep your focus to your mission and vision.

Visions are refined, not changed. Refine your vision, and revise your plan if necessary.

Don't sacrifice your character, personal relationships, or integrity for your vision. Learn to balance your life. Maintain your peace.

Never be afraid to fail because you can only succeed once you've failed a few times.

Biggest challenge?

Financial sustainability

Maintaining my life balance

Learning to celebrate my failures

TIPS FROM MOLLY MACDONALD, FOUNDER AND CEO OF THE PINK FUND

A few years ago, I met Molly MacDonald, the founder and CEO of The Pink Fund (pinkfund.org), a nonprofit that provides financial aid to breast cancer patients. The now 67-year-old breast cancer survivor was buzzing with energy as she told me about the charity she started in 2007, and her personal story triggering it. MacDonald's important work creating The Pink Fund got me thinking: it's not such an outlandish dream to start a nonprofit if you're over 50 and there's a genuine need, the way she did.

The Pink Fund provides aid to approved applicants to pay for things such as health insurance premiums and essentials like mortgage, rent, and car or utility payments. At the time of diagnosis, a woman must be employed and either have lost her job or be on leave due to the diagnosis and treatment. The fund disbursed more than a half million dollars ($566,648.13) in benefits in its fiscal year ending June 2018, 57% of which paid housing costs. As of April 8, 2019, the fund had distributed a little over $3.3 million.

MacDonald, who has a background in sales and marketing, launched her Beverly Hills, Michigan–based nonprofit after her own financial struggle during her treatment for and recovery from breast cancer. When diagnosed, she was on the cusp of starting a six-figure job, making her the family's primary breadwinner (her five children were then ages 12 to 21; her husband is a piano technician). Although the surgery and radiation left MacDonald cancer free, her prospective employer dropped its job offer due to her health condition.

The family's finances imploded and their home went into foreclosure. "I thought: 'Oh my gosh, we are going to be homeless,'" recalls MacDonald. "I was just stunned. I couldn't figure out how we were going to pick up the pieces."

Her "Divine Inspiration"

Then she had what she calls "divine inspiration." Says MacDonald: "If I could help one family from not experiencing this, it would make sense of what we were going through. Otherwise, I would end up feeling bitter."

So she bought Nolo's *Starting & Building a Nonprofit: A Practical Guide*, and, with her husband, began mapping plans. Within a year, The Pink Fund was born.

I asked MacDonald for her advice to others who are eager to launch nonprofits around causes that are dear to them. Here are 10 of her tips:

1. **Start out by volunteering your time.** "In the first three years, we worked from my kitchen table, raising about $30,000. By 2010, I had enough savings put aside that I quit my job [working for a mortgage company] and told the board that I would volunteer full time without pay for one year," MacDonald says. In 2011, the board voted MacDonald a $40,000 salary, which has since risen to more than $70,000.

2. **Go slow.** "It took a year to lay the groundwork to start the nonprofit," says MacDonald. Getting traction wasn't easy. "I have stood in rooms with three people listening to my spiel. There were times when I wanted to give up," she says.

"While people thought it was a great idea, they were not willing to put a big chunk of change behind it. They all said I was a big dreamer and would pooh-pooh it."

Some people will applaud your mission but will hang back before offering funding. "They don't want to get in your game until you are successful," says MacDonald. That's why, she says, "you've got to be in it for the long haul."

3. **Invite a well-known speaker for an event.** Bringing in someone with a following could gin up interest in your nonprofit when you're just starting out and under the radar.

"Once, we invited the author Kris Carr, who had written *Crazy Sexy Cancer Tips*, to speak at a luncheon," says MacDonald. "My idea was she had a huge tribe of followers who align with what we were doing. Well, we sold out; 400 people came. And now all of a sudden, these people who didn't know about The Pink Fund but loved Kris Carr knew about us. It allowed us to tell our story."

Turns out, the head of Ford's Warriors in Pink breast cancer charity was a Carr fan and called MacDonald when she heard about the upcoming luncheon, saying Ford wanted to help fund the event. Several months later, Ford invited The Pink Fund to join Warriors in Pink.

4. **Create a vision board to inspire you.** That's a collage on a big white poster board with images and magazine cutouts that home in on your dreams and goals for your nonprofit.

"I thought vision boards were a bunch of baloney," says MacDonald. "But in March of 2007, a year after I started The Pink Fund, I went to a breast cancer survivor's recovery conference and we were asked to create a poster board around professional life, family life, physical life, and spiritual life. I put the Ford blue oval logo on it; I knew they were one of the major corporate participants in breast cancer research and awareness and were located near me."

Fast-forward five years later when The Pink Fund became part of Ford's Warriors in Pink family. "That has been a game changer in terms of our credibility and ability to fundraise, and I believe that mental image I carried with me helped make that a reality," says MacDonald.

5. **Use your connections to get the word out through the media.** "When we were ready to launch, I got one of my former employers, the *Detroit Free*

(Continued)

TIPS FROM MOLLY MACDONALD, FOUNDER AND CEO OF THE PINK FUND (*Cont'd*)

Press, to run a story on our effort. More than a dozen newspapers picked it up and that's how people heard about it. Then, donations began to come in," she says.

6. **Seek out nonfinancial donations or barter for services.** "Our office space, legal work, brochure, and website are all donated. Even our logo was designed by one of my girlfriends in exchange for a table I gave her," says MacDonald.

7. **Make sure your financials are in good shape.** MacDonald says you need to run a lean organization. "Set up QuickBooks accounting software, file your taxes on time, and have a treasurer who advises you on how to spend money and live within your budget," she says. "Nonprofit means you're not making a profit, but you are a business. And you must run the organization with those principles."

8. **Develop an intern program.** "It's a win for both of you," says MacDonald. "It saves some costs, and you are able to give interns work experience for 10 weeks or so."

   Besides also getting to learn from them, the internship can pay off for your charity in other ways. "We get interns through arrangements with two local colleges and have recently aligned with a college that has a patient navigation program, who will help us seek out other resources to help patients," says MacDonald.

9. **Use social media relentlessly.** "Follow people [on Facebook, LinkedIn, and Twitter] you respect and learn from them," says MacDonald. "I have made amazing connections that way."

10. **Network, network, network.** "Attend community events and volunteer to speak at local Rotary Clubs and organizations like that. You never know who you will meet," says MacDonald.

Or where your networking will lead.

Case in point: When her daughter was working for Diane von Furstenberg, MacDonald was asked to model as a survivor for the designer's fashion show benefit for the Susan G. Komen organization. "Someone from the SEED Foundation read about it and sent us a check for $5,000 with a note that said, 'Let me know if you need more.' Since then, this woman has given us probably $125,000 and is looking at making a more significant gift," says MacDonald.

Then there was the small function that MacDonald thought wasn't a great use of her time to attend. She went anyway. "While I was there, I was introduced to a woman who has raised $42 million in the nonprofit world. Now I'm meeting with her in two weeks," says MacDonald. And that could wind up helping more women with breast cancer who could use a hand.

Chapter Recap

In this chapter, we learned about two women who launched non-profits that spoke to their hearts and life experiences. They each have different paths, but much of the advice is similar: take your time, find your niche, and ask for help.

YOUR TO-DO LIST

- Journal about how you might make a difference with a small nonprofit start-up. What causes do you wear on your sleeve?
- Volunteer your time at similar organizations that you would like as a model for your venture.
- Create a vision board to inspire you.

Food, Glorious Food

Doug Rauch, Daily Table

By 2008 Doug Rauch, president of Trader Joe's, was cooked. He had spent the last three decades – practically his whole career – orchestrating the eccentric California retailer's speedy expansion to the East Coast, developing its purchasing program and private-label food business while traveling "ceaselessly." He was just 56. Making money was no longer a priority, and he wanted to tap the brakes and "get off the wheel," as he put it when I interviewed him for *Forbes*.

So Rauch "retired" with a scheme to keep active, serving on corporate and nonprofit boards from his base in Newton, Massachusetts. It only took a few months before he realized that he had "too much operational stuff in my blood" to be contented with that.

Rauch had learned about a program at Harvard University called the Advanced Leadership Initiative (ALI; advancedleadership.harvard.edu), a yearlong program for executives and other successful professionals, mostly in their 50s and 60s, looking to take on major social troubles or move into the nonprofit world. The handpicked fellows devote a calendar year auditing classes across the entire university, brainstorming with professors and other students, making contacts, and creating their own solo projects.

In 2009, Rauch applied to the program, knowing he wanted to do something that was immersive and had a social impact. He also reckoned that he had the best shot at bringing about change if he stuck to what he understood. "I really do know the food system, and I know retail," he told me. Plus, he'd long been troubled by both food waste and the problems poor people have affording nutritious food.

Rauch earned his undergraduate degree in 1972 at Cal State Los Angeles. And in 1991 (14 years into his career with Trader Joe's) he attained an Executive MBA at the Peter Drucker School of Management at Claremont University. Says Rauch, "Peter was still alive and teaching, and I enjoyed many conversations with him (he was a shopper at TJ's)." He entered Harvard in January 2010 and spent the next year studying a range of subjects from dark matter (in his astronomy class) to agribusiness and social entrepreneurship through an array of courses. About once per week he joined three-hour dialogue sessions or dinners focused on change leadership with other institute fellows. To his delight, he was offered a "Senior Fellow" second year at Harvard and accepted. "I got to double my enjoyment of working with faculty and students while honing my Daily Table model. I left the ALI program in December 2011.

"Going back to college was a blast," says Rauch, now 66. "I soaked up the pure joy of learning and the energy of young people. I began to look at the world with fresh eyes. I was re-energized." That inspiration also pushed him to reconsider his food-market concept numerous times as he "bounced ideas off of and crowdsourced with really smart people."

Today, Rauch is headfirst into his next act. In 2015 he opened Daily Table (dailytable.org), a 3,500-square-foot nonprofit market in the lower-income Dorchester neighborhood of Boston. Today it sells groceries and produce at ultra-low prices and healthy cooked and ready-to-serve meals at prices intended to vie with the cheapest fast-food restaurants. It also offers free cooking classes in a teaching kitchen.

Daily Table keeps prices low, largely by accepting tax-deductible donations of perishable food near its expiration date or close to being too ripe. Donors include local growers, wholesalers, and manufacturers like Amazon Fresh, Cedar's (maker of hummus and other Mediterranean foods), Chobani, Hain Celestial, Ready Pac Salad, and organic-yogurt maker Stonyfield Farm.

It's an ingenious concept: selling food that might end up in trash containers. But "sell by," "use by," and "best before" dates account for a big chunk of the $165 billion of food wasted in the U.S. each year, according to a study by researchers from Harvard Law School and the Natural Resources Defense Council. And Rauch certainly has collected a top-notch list of funders including PepsiCo Foundation, Newman's Own Foundation, and Robert Wood Johnson Foundation, among others.

There are Daily Table stores in Dorchester along with a slightly larger one (4,500 square feet of retail space) in Roxbury, another economically challenged part of Boston's inner city. And Daily Table is looking for additional stores in Boston and beyond. "With funding, we'd love to expand to other communities around the country," says Rauch.

Daily Table now has over 42,000 members (membership is required by IRS, but is open to all free of charge). "We move approximately a million nutritional servings into the community each month," Rauch told me.

Rauch had the honor of winning the James Beard Foundation Leadership Award in 2018 for the work he's done with Daily Table. And the stores were featured (the only retail solution mentioned) in Anthony Bourdain's documentary, *Wasted! The Story of Food Waste.* "But it's the stories our customers share with us each day that means the most to me – how we're making a difference in their, and their kids', lives," Rauch said.

The whole Daily Table operation, he explained to me, "is really a healthcare initiative masquerading as a healthy food store. I believe in my heart that most of us find real satisfaction in our lives when we are doing something meaningful," says Rauch.

Making It Work

I asked Doug to look back and share his thoughts on starting a nonprofit.

Kerry: What did starting your own nonprofit mean to you personally?

Doug: It meant I once again had a compelling purpose to my daily routine. I was engaged in something bigger than myself. And it meant that I was putting my time and reputation on the line. People counted on me – foundations counted on me – to open these stores successfully and make a contribution. I had to deliver. When I received our first donation ($75,000 from Blue Cross Blue Shield) I looked at the check and said, "Okay, Doug. Now there's no turning back on this idea. You have to see it through."

Were you confident that you were doing the right thing? Any second-guessing?

How can you second-guess any effort that helps fight hunger or food insecurity? No way. What I constantly question is if there's a better way to do it – how can we be better every day? I second-guess the reason why the richest nation in the world has 1 in 7 people that are nutritionally hungry – unable to eat decent, healthy food just because of economics. I wonder what we're thinking to allow 17 million kids to grow up hungry? And how few people know about this or care. That's worth second-guessing.

Anything you would have done differently?

Yep. I would have realized that this was going to kick my ass. What was I thinking? Tackling major social challenges means dealing with systemic problems with no single vector solution. There are no quick fixes, no trick moves. You can't just outsmart the problem. And you definitely can't just keep doing what we've been doing – that's clearly not removing the problem. In short, I would have known that I needed more capital, more capacity from the beginning to really do this right. And that it wouldn't be a quick fix!

How do you measure your success?

How much healthy food are we moving into the community? Because we deal primarily with economically challenged customers, we know that if they buy something they'll eat it. (They may not buy it a second time, but they'll definitely eat what they buy). And since there is not a single item at Daily Table that doesn't meet strict nutritional standards set by a world-class group of dietitians here in Boston, we're confident that our "output" can count as "outcome." Food purchased equals healthy food consumed. We also have two other minor measures: how much food did we recover that would have been in a landfill (now over 4 million pounds recovered); and second, how close are we to hitting economic sustainability (we're at 67% currently).

How did your preparation help you succeed?

My career at Trader Joe's was of course essential, but the Harvard Fellowship allowed me to dive deeply into the nonprofit world of "theory of change" lingo – and the very different world that nonprofits live in.

What do you tell other people who ask for your advice?

Find something that you're passionate about, that uses your talents, and makes a difference in the world. Don't waste your time chasing happiness – that's a fool's errand. Instead focus on living a purposeful life of meaning. Happiness is not to be pursued … it ensues from a purpose-driven life. Oh, and know that if you want to tackle a major social challenge, it will take much longer, and be much harder, than whatever you thought!

What books or resources did you use or recommend others to use?

While I'm a fan of a written education, I honestly found speaking with others more meaningful – people already engaged in the field. What had they learned? What would they do differently? What isn't being dealt with properly? I sought those I admired that could teach me.

What are some of the unexpected rewards and surprises?

It's far more satisfying than I expected knowing that although our impact to date is limited, to each customer we really matter in their life. And I guess I was surprised by how much others are willing to step up and help, as well as how grateful a community is when you treat them with respect and provide a hand up, not a handout.

Lessons learned?

Where to start? Don't silo, ask for help, be vulnerable and open even if it hurts to see the pain around us, give a damn and do something – almost anything – about it, and do it all as service of the greater good.

Biggest challenge?

Funding. We don't fit neatly into many foundations' program boxes. We try to take a systems approach, and it turns out there aren't that many foundations that reward that effort. Also, we were late in the game to recognize that we are a fundraising organization – and will be for some time (even if it's at reduced percent of revenue).

STEPS TO FINDING PURPOSE IN YOUR NEW BUSINESS

Here are the steps you can take – preferably before you retire from your old job – to find new work with purpose in your next chapter.

Get financially fit. Debt is a dream killer – one of my favorite mantras. If you're financially fit, it gives you options. You're nimble enough to try things out, or work for less than you did in the past, for the reward of loving what you do and knowing you're having an impact on the world around you.

Shape up. To fight ageism in the workplace, you must have the stamina for a new beginning; you need to be physically in shape and stick to a healthy diet. You don't have to bench-press heavy weights or run fast miles, mind you, but you do need to have a level of fitness. It will show. You will exude energy and a can-do, positive vibe. People will want what you have.

Take time to reflect. "Carve out solitude, space, and time to consider what issues and roles speak to you," says Marci Alboher, author of *The Encore Career Handbook*. You need a certain amount of humility to switch to nonprofit work. There's a shared sense of the mission, a collaborative decision-making environment. If you're used to being an independent worker or a leader, this might not be a suitable fit without an attitude adjustment.

Do an inventory of your existing skills and interests. How can you redeploy your financial expertise, for example, or your tech know-how or management skills on a new path? Rauch redeployed his knowledge of the food retail industry.

Consider working with a career or life coach to talk through steps needed to make the shift. Successful career shifters typically set flexible time frames of three to five years to move into a new field. Finding what you want to do next is a process, so be patient.

Hit the books. Return to school for a tune-up or a skills refresh. In addition to the Harvard Advanced Leadership Initiative that Rauch attended, the Stanford Distinguished Careers Institute (dci.stanford.edu) offers a program for professionals in their 50s, 60s, and beyond.

There are also encore career centers at Notre Dame and the University of Texas. Notre Dame's Irish Angel Network of high-risk investors reviews social enterprise pitches its fellows develop.

The University of Minnesota offers an Advanced Careers Initiative. A few shorter programs are less expensive: the Encore Transition Program at Union Theological Seminary in New York City, the Encore Hamline Fellows at Hamline College in St. Paul, Minnesota, and Encore!Connecticut at the University of Connecticut in Hartford and Fairfield counties. Encore!Connecticut, a 16-week fellowship program, begun by the University of Connecticut's Nonprofit Leadership Program, helps corporate professionals, mostly over 50, convert their corporate expertise to the nonprofit world. It includes a crash course in nonprofit management and finance held in local nonprofits and a two-month, 30-hour-per-week fellowship at a local nonprofit.

Be practical, though, when it comes to outlays on education. If possible, take some classes while your current employer is still offering tuition reimbursement (though be sure to investigate whether there's a payback requirement if you leave).

You might easily be able to hone your existing skills for the nonprofit sector with just a course or two, such as accounting for nonprofits. (Seton Hall University maintains a searchable list of nonprofit management courses across the country: http://academic.shu.edu/npo/help.php.)

Subscribe to *The Chronicle of Philanthropy.* Read its articles, and follow the thought leaders in the sector of the industry you're interested in on LinkedIn and Twitter.

(Continued)

STEPS TO FINDING PURPOSE IN YOUR NEW BUSINESS (*Cont'd*)

Write your nonprofit-oriented resume and LinkedIn profile. Your resume and professional profile must show what experience and skills you have and how it relates to the organization you're interested in launching. Tell your story, your passion – why you, why this cause?

Volunteer. If there's an organization whose mission calls to you, raise your hand. "Get out of your head and into the world," says Alboher. Look into volunteer opportunities to start developing some in-depth experience in an area that interests you and taps into your expertise. Serve on a board.

This builds your network and gets people to start thinking of you in new ways, while giving you an insight into how these organizations run. Volunteering can also freshen your skills and stretch new muscles to spur ideas for your own start-up.

To find organizations where you might get involved, check out websites such as Commongood Careers (commongoodcareers.org) and the Bridgespan Group (Bridgespan.org). Other helpful sites include BoardnetUSA.org, the Points of Light HandsOn network (www.pointsoflight.org/handsonnetwork), Idealist.org, and Volunteermatch.org. AARP (AARP.org) also has a "Volunteer Wizard" match-up board. Look around your community. Where might you lend a hand?

Do some pro bono consulting. Take on a consulting assignment for a local charity gratis. This helps you ramp up your knowledge about how nonprofits run.

Connect with your network. Whom do you know in the nonprofit field? Tap your LinkedIn and other social media connections to search for possible contacts. Book an advice and counseling lunch or coffee to brainstorm. Always ask for another name or two of people you might be able to reach out to for guidance.

Polish your elevator speech. Funders want to hear why you want this specific job for this specific cause and how it resonates with your personal story. Your passion and commitment for the organization and cause are the things that set you apart from other candidates. Getting good at explaining this is crucial. Wear your heart on your sleeve.

Chapter Recap

In this chapter, we learned how one man was able to redeploy his decades-long food industry expertise to start a nonprofit in the same arena. He took his time developing his plan, headed back to campus to hone his concept before launching, and added the necessary blueprint to help him launch successfully.

YOUR TO-DO LIST

- Look into educational opportunities to ramp up your knowledge of the nonprofit world.
- Network to connect with individuals who can teach you from their experience.
- Start an exercise program if you don't already have one. This transition could "kick your ass," Rauch says. Engaging in something bigger than yourself takes stamina.

Hope in Harlem

Jamal Joseph, Impact Repertory Theatre
Courtesy of Encore.org / Talking Eyes Media.

Jamal Joseph stood powerlessly on the Harlem pavement. He was outside his apartment building in 1997, watching a ring of women mourn, cry, and comfort the mother of a 16-year-old boy, who had been shot and murdered.

The adolescent had lived next door. "He was a good kid, who was defending his sister," says Joseph, now 65 and a professor of Professional Practice at Columbia University School of the Arts in the Film Department. "There were several other men with me, and all we could do is watch the women cry," he says. "I thought, I have got to do something right here in this community to make a change."

The year was 1997, and Harlem was like "a prison without bars," Joseph says. "The crack epidemic was ravaging the community and buildings were crumbling. It was like a powder keg," he said. "And that was when I decided to create an organization to help young people understand there are other ways out, other options, other tools."

I met Joseph in 2015 when he was awarded a cash prize of $25,000 in recognition and support of his work. He was one of that year's six winners of the Purpose Prize, then awarded to Americans 60 and older who have had an impact on the world.

The award was created by Encore.org, a nonprofit that has spent 20 years building a movement to tap the skills and experience of those in mid-life and beyond to improve communities. Its current efforts center on the Gen2Gen (generationtogeneration.org) campaign to rally one million adults 50+ to stand up for – and with – young people today to improve life for all. As Encore.org founder Marc Freedman likes to say, "The fountain *of* youth is the fountain *with* youth."

Joseph's idea for his organization came from his firsthand understanding of how ruthless it could be on the streets. He had grown up in foster care and was a 15-year-old Bronx honor student when he joined the Black Panthers in Harlem in 1968.

A year later he was in a group of Panthers who were blamed for plotting to blow up police station houses and the New York Botanical Garden in the Bronx. Joseph's case was separated from the others because he was a minor and he was not tried on the charges.

In 1981, however, Joseph was charged with involvement in the theft of a Brink's armored car in Rockland County, New York, in which two police officers and a guard were killed. He was acquitted of participating in the robbery but convicted of helping a fellow suspect hide.

In the federal penitentiary in Leavenworth, Kansas, where he served 5½ years, Joseph wrote his first play, received two degrees, and created a theater group. He saw how plays brought together prisoners from all parts of the yard, previously segregated along racial lines, to write and produce plays jointly. That experience led to his subsequent career as a filmmaker and playwright. He began teaching when he got out and ultimately became a professor at Columbia.

"I saw the power of art to bring people from different cultures together to tell their stories, and to heal," he said. "Guys who grew up distrusting each other, hating each other, were sharing stories and creating."

In response to the heartbreaking Harlem scene that day, Joseph founded the Impact Repertory Theatre (impactreptheatre.org), a nonprofit performing-arts group for teenagers, with his wife, Joyce, and Voza Rivers, the executive producer and founding member of the New Heritage Theatre Group (newheritagetheatre.org), the oldest black nonprofit theater company in New York City.

His idea: to offer a safe place that emphasizes discipline and commitment, where kids could talk and write about their own lives – from bullying and gangs to violence and drugs. And then they'd find ways to translate their experiences into dance movements, plays, poems, rap, and songs. In essence, they'd learn a technique to use their imagination as a tool to change their neighborhood.

Nine kids showed up for the first gathering in the basement of a community center in Harlem.

Since that first meeting, more than 1,500 kids ranging in age from 12 to 18 have participated in Impact workshops, performances, and community service in New York. (More than 4,000 youth have participated in Impact-led workshops at schools and community centers in New York, Philadelphia, and Atlanta.) They perform at a range of stages, from the Apollo Theater, Lincoln Center, and the United Nations to schools, homeless shelters, and prisons.

After auditioning, students accepted into the group join a mandatory three-month boot camp that teaches leadership skills, conflict resolution, and time management, as well as civic engagement. "We're not looking for talent, but kids who are willing to *try*," Joseph told me when I initially interviewed him for *The New York Times*.

There is no fee for the program, but "it's not free – you pay for it with your dedication and hard work, commitment to the program, and to others," he says.

Boot campers are required to partake in routine community service and keep their grades up; they also write journals and participate in regular exercise.

After boot camp ends, the group meets for six hours each Saturday at the School of the Arts at Columbia University to review what's going on in the community and in their lives, rehearse dance routines, and take part in writing workshops.

About 75% of Impact youth who stay with the organization through high school graduate and go on to universities such as Brown, Fordham, Howard, and Yale.

"When we started Impact it was, how do you maintain hope in a Harlem where buildings are crumbling and it looks like a war zone, where there were gunshots every night?" says Joseph. "How do you let kids know that their lives are important, and they matter, and there is hope?"

But the focus has changed. "Now it's how do you keep hope in the community where kids are growing up around the corner from million-dollar condos and bistros and fancy restaurants that they pass on the way to school?" he says. "How do you maintain hope when the disparity is right in front of you?"

Another of Joseph's efforts is an intergenerational program for youth and older adults in the Harlem community, who regularly meet and connect with the Impact students to share experiences. "A lot of these kids are being raised by grandparents, so it makes sense to learn from each other, share stories, and moments of inspiration," Joseph says.

For example, on one occasion the students spent time talking about the realities of racism with Janet Langhart Cohen, 77, an author, and the wife of former secretary of defense William S. Cohen, about her play *Anne and Emmett,* which imagines a conversation between Anne Frank, the 16-year-old Jewish girl killed by the Nazis, and Emmett Till, the 14-year-old black teen whose murder in 1950s Mississippi over accusations of whistling at a white woman helped spark the civil rights movement.

"My greatest reward is knowing I helped create a space where young people can see amazing possibilities for themselves, for their communities, and for the world. We're giving kids the power to perform not just around stages of New York, but in life," says Joseph, who does not get paid for his service. "This is my calling."

And although he was free to spend the cash award from the Purpose Prize however he chose, Joseph invested that windfall back into his organization.

"What characterizes so many of the Purpose Prize winners [now AARP's Purpose Prize] is not only entrepreneurial thinking, but they're also pragmatic problem solvers, as opposed to wild-eyed idealists," says Freedman, founder and CEO of Encore.org. "They are practical idealists."

The trigger for their efforts, as it was for Joseph, is typically "an immediate challenge in front of them that is specific and discreet that they are trying to address, and ultimately it unfolds into a sustained and significant project," says Freedman.

Many of the people who have won the Purpose Prize have struggled in their lives, and, in many cases, failed, Freedman told me. "They are people who have had ups and downs and don't have considerable financial resources, who are working in local settings," he says. "Everyone was talking about how innovative and entrepreneurial young people were. We wanted to show there was an undiscovered continent of innovation and idealism in the older population that could be just as powerful a force for society as the work being done by people in their 20s."

Freedman sees a coming together of the generations: "It is not only older people working on behalf of younger generations, but coming together with younger generations to try to solve difficult intractable problems in society," he says. "Like Jamal, they are connecting with young people to do this work together, which is so much more real."

For Joseph, it's a "tremendous honor as a prize winner to have been invited into the space of people using their bonus years to make a difference," he says. It confirms some advice he gleaned decades ago from his own mentor, singer and actor Harry Belafonte, 88, that has clung to him.

"I was young and worried about a script I was writing and raising the money for it. Mr. Belafonte said, 'Don't worry about the money. Do good work, and what's supposed to follow will follow.'"

Making It Work

I asked Jamal to look back and share his thoughts on starting a nonprofit.

> **Kerry: What did starting your own nonprofit mean to you personally?**
>
> **Jamal:** It was exciting and challenging. I wasn't quite sure how to make it all work, but I knew Harlem was in a critical moment in terms of the need for leadership

programs, creative arts education, and mentorship for young people. I had an interesting combination of experiences that went into creating an organization that addressed all three of those issues.

Were you confident that you were doing the right thing? Any second-guessing?

I was confident I was doing the right thing and even though I was older, starting Impact was a coming-of-age moment. I had been a member of the Black Panther Party, part of other community organizations, and worked for various not-for-profits – but was never the founder or executive director.

Anything you would have done differently?

We started Impact without any real funding. We didn't think there was time to create a model, write proposals, and then launch six months to two years later – we were motivated by the urgency of the moment. I wished (and still wish) we had a better development infrastructure.

How do you measure your success?

We measure success by the number of young people who come in the door wanting to be actors, singers, and dancers and head off to college to study science, math, technology, education, social work, anthropology, business (the list goes on) – "creative scholars," who know the arts will always enrich their lives but have additional goals.

We are also proud our entire leadership and teaching staff are Impact alumni who went to college and are now volunteering at the program.

How did your preparation help you succeed?

My grassroots training taught me to listen and take leadership from the people you were there to serve. My academic training taught me to be well prepared. My artistic training taught me to be fully present in the moment and be willing to throw everything out the window and improvise.

What do you tell other people who ask for your advice?

Immerse yourself in what you want to do. Volunteer, apprentice, shadow those inspirational leaders who are doing the work. I've learned so much.

What books or resources did you use or recommend others to use?

Two of my favorite books are *The Autobiography of Malcolm X* and *Jonathan Livingston Seagull.* Both are about transformation. My greatest life lesson has been that love truly has the power to change individuals, communities, nations, and the world.

What are some of the unexpected rewards and surprises?

I am always running into young adults in their 20s and 30s who will hug me and remind me that they were an Impact kid and that they are now college grads working in a variety of fields. Many are doing some form of mentoring. A few are now parents who tell me they're going to bring their children to Impact when they're older.

Biggest challenge?

Raising enough money to continue and grow the program. Twenty years, 2,000 alumni, and an ocean of amazing memories later, we still have a lot to learn about development and fundraising.

Lessons learned?

Everything I've learned is embodied by my personal mantra: "There's no start date on activism and no expiration date on dreams."

■　■　■

PS: If you want to meet Jamal virtually, I recommend that you check out this video: youtu.be/D3axJGVS1PI.

SO YOU WANT TO START A NONPROFIT

Starting a nonprofit can be a particularly byzantine process, but the payout can be genuinely gratifying. One of the principal resources to help you get rolling is Idealist (idealist.org).

This website provides detailed direction, lays out initial steps for launching a new entity, and delivers resources. According to Idealist, normally you will know you have a solid case for starting a new nonprofit if:

- you have a clientele or beneficiary with a bona fide need that's not being met by a current nonprofit or program,
- you have a pioneering programming idea or approach to meeting the need, and
- you already have (or know how you can attain) the financial and in-kind donations needed to support the organization for the conceivable future.

You have the passion, but do you have what it takes to really get this dream off the ground? The answer may be *absolutely,* if you have done the following:

- You have methodically researched the industry and field you are entering and have a concrete plan of action.
- You have spent gobs of time understanding the world of nonprofits, being out in the community getting your hands dirty, so to speak, by working with other nonprofits, and interacting with those social entrepreneurs who have already started nonprofits to collect their perspective and knowledge.
- You have finished the IRS paperwork for forming a nonprofit entity. IRS Publication 557 (www.irs.gov/publications/p557) contains information on all the organizational categories and instructions on qualifying for and applying for 501(c) status.
- You have the backing to launch your company and support it for a sufficient period.

Chapter Recap

In this chapter, we learned how a man who understood the barriers youth face growing up in Harlem, and the challenges of breaking out of the cycle of violence, took action to start a nonprofit from scratch to use the power and positivity of the arts to deliver hope and a new path to success.

YOUR TO-DO LIST

- Look around your immediate town and city, or where you grew up. Is there a pressing issue you can help solve? Is there a way to bring about change to help at-risk children by bringing adults together with them to work toward solutions?
- Look for possible donors or funders in your community. Are there any people or organization leaders who you might be able to approach with your concept for input and potential backing?
- Read through IRS Publication 557 to learn the ins and outs of setting up a not-for-profit entity.

CHAPTER

The Magic of Music

Belle Mickelson, Dancing with the Spirit
Courtesy of Encore.org / Talking Eyes Media.

Keep on the sunny side, always on the sunny side,
Keep on the sunny side of life
It will help us every day, it will brighten all the way,
If we'll keep on the sunny side of life

When I hear these lines from the song "Keep on the Sunny Side," I can't help but picture another one of the Purpose Prize winners, Belle Mickelson, now 71, a science teacher turned Episcopal priest, who lives in Cordova, Alaska.

Mickelson is keen on the fiddle and education. And it's that mighty mixture that encouraged her to start a nonprofit in 2006, Dancing with the Spirit (dancingwiththespirit.org), based in Fairbanks. The organization aims to connect children and elders through music.

Her staff is primarily Alaska Native, but includes her 35-year-old son, Mike, a talented bluegrass musician. "This program has been such a blessing for my family," Belle says. "Often you start out thinking you're going to help others – but they give you so much more than you could have ever dreamed! We have met so many wonderful people in the villages whose stories have changed our lives for the better."

Mickelson's roving music program currently teaches youth living in 53 remote villages across Alaska – songs from bluegrass to country, folk and rock 'n' roll. They range from "Eagle Island Blues," an Athabascan love song, to tunes like "Keep on the Sunny Side" and "Jambalaya," which was written and recorded by American country music singer Hank Williams. Johnny Cash songs are other favorites. High school students bring songs that they want to learn along, too.

The mission statement says it all: "Dancing with the Spirit connects youth and elders through school music programs and camps – promoting spiritual, physical, and mental wellness with the joy, love, and hope of music. Our goal is to prevent suicide, drug, alcohol, and domestic abuse by building self-esteem, preserving musical traditions, and encouraging strong healthy communities."

Talk about a bold, audacious endeavor.

The outfit's school programs consist of week-long classes in singing, guitar, ukulele, fiddle, mandolin, banjo, bass, square dancing, and Native culture. Mickelson and her team invite community elders, local musicians, and teachers to tutor alongside them and encourage students to sing in their Native languages. The instruments are marked with colored dots to represent guitar chords and lines to mark where the fiddle fingers go, making it easier to get the hang of it. The words and notes of the songs themselves are sketched out on large notepads so everyone can sing and play together.

The goal is that by the end of the week, the elementary school students can play 15 songs on the guitar and several on the fiddle. High school students can play double that many – even though they may never have played before, according to Mickelson.

To date, the Dancing with the Spirit team has spread their magic and music in Alaganuk, Allakaket, Angoon, Anvik, Arctic Village, Beaver, Chalkyitsik, Chenega, Circle, Coffman Cove, Eagle, Emmonak, Fort Yukon, Galena, Grayling, Hollis, Holy Cross, Hooper Bay, Hughes, Huslia, Hydaburg, Hyder, Kaltag, Kasaan, Kivalina,

Kotzebue, Koyukuk, Manley Hot Springs, McGrath, Mentasta Lake, Minto, Naukati, Nikolai, Northway, Nuiqsut, Nulato, Pelican, Point Hope, Port Alexander, Rampart, Ruby, Scammon Bay, Shageluk, Stevens Village, Tanacross, Tanana, Tetlin, Thorne Bay, Tok, Unalakleet, Venetie, Whale Pass, and Yakutat.

Phew. You get the picture. Last year they spent 37 weeks in village schools. That's a lot of miles and lives touched. Dancing with the Spirit has also helped organize camps in the larger communities of Fairbanks, Anchorage, Juneau, Kodiak, and Cordova.

When I met Mickelson she had just received a $25,000 Purpose Prize for Intergenerational Impact, sponsored by the Eisner Foundation (eisnerfoundation.org), and she was beaming. To say she exudes joy is an understatement. She's one of those people you meet in life who you can't say exactly what it is, but you know in your heart, you simply want to be around to feel her warmth and energy. It rubs off on you.

Mickelson, who grew up in Lima, Ohio, and started playing the violin at the age of 10, still has the little cigar box of rocks she gathered on her family trip to Alaska in 1962, when they drove up the Alcan Highway on a summer holiday.

Little did she know that decades later, she would spend more than a third of the year flying in teeny three-to-nine-seater airplanes, laden with as many as 30 fiddles, guitars, and ukuleles plus boxes of healthy treats to small, far-flung villages. Although their mission is to teach schoolchildren how to play songs traditionally sung in their village alongside their elders in week-long school music camps, it is much more than that. It's a deeper life change that she's after.

Her background prepared her for this stage of her life: Mickelson had run an alternative high school for two years and taught sixth grade. She'd operated a commercial fisheries program for high school and college students in Cordova, taught marine-education teacher workshops statewide for the University of Alaska, and helped start the Cordova 4H Music Camp.

But one day she traveled to Galena, a remote Athabascan village with a population of around 500, located along the Yukon River, 270 air miles west of Fairbanks, to conduct a fisheries workshop. When it was over, she was asked to an elder's house for a jam session to play guitar and fiddle, and afterward, while drinking tea, she asked her hosts, 'How's it going?' "They told me how depressed and sad they were," she recalls. "There were so many teen suicides in the community. At that point, I thought, 'What could I do as one person?'"

She later found the answer. Healing with music was "engindered" in her, as my own grandmother might say. From the moment she took up playing the violin, at the age of 10, music has been her passion. "I always thought of it as a kind of hobby, until as a science teacher I looked at the impact music had on kids, especially in the alternative high school where I taught," Mickelson says. "Almost every kid had had some major tragedy in their lives. The way we got them back on track is with music and art. We taught them to play the ukulele, to play the guitar. Once they gained confidence with music, then they could tackle English and math."

But before she could launch her traveling music camps, Mickelson decided on a personal career shift and entered seminary to become an Episcopal priest. She was ordained in 2007, and soon after became the rector at St. George's Episcopal Church in Cordova, a small but lively parish whose average attendance is 21.

As a priest, she travels to villages not only to teach music, but to sometimes bring religious services and support to communities in the evenings and on weekends. Her vital goal, however, is to beat back the depression often sparked by, or masked through, alcohol and drug abuse by teenagers in the towns. "You can't just say don't do something; you need to replace it with something," Mickelson says.

"The great part about music is we will have a roomful of kids and they all listen to each other. They sing. When they're dancing, they're reaching out their hand to grab another person's hand, and they are looking them in the eye and smiling. Music builds community and makes the elders so happy!"

Making It Work

I asked Belle to look back and share her thoughts on starting a nonprofit.

> **Kerry: What did starting your own nonprofit mean to you personally?**
>
> Belle: I really like what someone with the Indigenous Theological Institute said to me at the beginning. "It won't be anything like what you are expecting – but it will be even more wonderful."

Were you confident that you were doing the right thing? Any second-guessing?

Yes. I asked for guidance and input from local people. They have the knowledge and wisdom to guide you. Prayers are great, too.

Anything you would have done differently?

Encourage grant writers to join our team.

How do you measure your success?

Schools and tribes keep funding us and inviting us back to their villages year after year. In 2017, they spent $235,000 for 37 school music weeks including the costs for transportation and freight – plus at least another $28,000 for musical instruments.

How did your preparation help you succeed?

I knew the importance of building on your compassion, hope, love, and faith – with an openness to many points of view. Find the goodness in everyone – and support them.

What do you tell other people who ask for your advice?

Listen and hang out with the elders!

What books or resources did you use or recommend others to use?

Talk personally to those you plan to help and get their recommendations.

What are some of the unexpected rewards and surprises?

People are out there praying for you to come and help them. When you answer that call, you'll be blessed beyond anything you can ever imagine.

Lessons learned?

Start something – and you'll be amazed at the results.

Biggest challenge?

Funding.

■ ■ ■

PS: If you want to meet Mickelson virtually, I recommend that you check out this lovely video: youtube.com/watch?v=YZNaL4_yGO4&feature=youtu.be.

WHAT IT REALLY TAKES TO LAUNCH A NONPROFIT FROM A PERSONAL PERSPECTIVE

- You can have all the moving pieces in place, funding to back your dream project, the tax laws carefully followed, and your mission firmly in place, but there's far more to starting a nonprofit entity than meets the eye. It's the inner challenges you must pay attention to and be aware of to make this a reality.
- The work to start and run a nonprofit is demanding physically and mentally. You're leading a charge in a new direction with fewer resources than you may have had at your disposal in other jobs you've held. This is not a day job. It's a commitment to long days and paltry pay. It's an all-heart-in commitment to change. And it can never be about your personal financial reward. It's the psychic reward. And only you will be in charge of that return.
- It can be a solitary pursuit. Yes, nonprofits are collaborative, and the team you assemble will pull together to work toward the goals of your organization, but tangible pats on the back and milestones of public recognition are not to be expected. Success comes in tiny steps, gradually over years.
- This is not a move for introverts. Can you say "charisma"? Skip the "I'm shy" excuse. You are the face of the organization. People will be drawn to you and your message, but that has a flip side to it. That kind of public exposure requires a thick skin at times and putting yourself out there on a regular basis. As the founder of a nonprofit, you're typically the face of the organization. But it is never about you. It's about the organization and its mission. Yes, it might be your calling, but it's the work you do that is the essence.
- Are you comfortable making the big "ask" of your circle of community, from close pals to family to those you only know tangentially? You might be asking for their time, a financial contribution, their willingness to help you share your mission and the nonprofit's story. And importantly, you might need to simply ask them to hold your hands on those dark days, when funding is sparse and you worry you can never accomplish what you've set out to do. You will need to be at ease asking friends, relatives, and community.

- Being the founder is all-consuming, especially when you are in the start-up phase. Be aware that it's far too easy to lose "you" in the process. It's not unusual to lose your own identity as your world becomes absorbed by creating and sustaining your dream. Create a boundary. You will thank yourself in years to come. And set aside time for you. A time for some quiet reflection each day, or planned days doing something away from your work. This is a key step in Kerry's fitness plan, of course. You need to be spiritually fit. Not in a religious sense necessarily, but it helps to have a meditation, yoga, or tai chi practice where you can regularly step away for balance and centering time. It can be as simple as walking your dog, but make the time to do this. It's key to your mental and physical health.

Fundraising Is Not for Wimps

How are you at picking up the phone and asking for money? All the great ideas and your passion for change and making a difference are well and good and exciting, but can you raise the funds to make it a reality? Be honest. This is the toughest step and it never seems to end. Even nonprofits that have been up and running for a decade or more bump up against this persistent and ever-present demand for having the resources to keep things afloat. Fundraising is a full-time job.

Those who are good at it know that it is a process of steadily building donor relationships over time. Yes, you might get some start-up funds, but that's just the tip of it. You need to create a pipeline or a range of sources. It requires creating trust and being able to show a return on their investment in you and your vision – even a tiny sliver of impact in your community can be huge. Over time you will build a database of donors and prospects, but this can never be set aside if you want to stay afloat.

One key is to not take all of this on yourself. Reach out and find volunteers who share your passion to help spread the message and raise money. You need to train them too, because they will be representatives of you and your nonprofit in the world. Be willing to hire help, even part time, to help you write grant proposals, run email and phone campaigns, manage fundraising events, and more.

Websites That Can Help

The Association of Fundraising Professionals (afpnet.org) represents over 33,000 members in 241 chapters throughout the world, working to generate philanthropic support for a variety of charitable organizations by offering its members training courses, certification programs, and more.

The Foundation Center (foundationcenter.org) educates thousands of people each year through a full curriculum of training courses, in the classroom

(Continued)

WHAT IT REALLY TAKES TO LAUNCH A NONPROFIT FROM A PERSONAL PERSPECTIVE (*Cont'd*)

and online. Free and affordable classes nationwide cover grant proposal writing and fundraising skills. The center also maintains databases of information on the foundations, corporate donors, and grant-making public charities in the United States and their recent grants.

The site consists of a variety of free search tools, tutorials, downloadable reports, and other information updated daily, including the Philanthropy News Digest, its daily news service. The foundation also offers webinars ranging from basic primers on fundraising to winning grants.

Take a Course in Fundraising

One way to whet your fundraising skills is to enroll in classes and webinars offered by the Foundation Center and the Association of Fundraising Professionals. Many community colleges and universities also offer courses in fundraising. The AFP (afpglobal.org/e-courses), for example, offers introductory-level e-courses that cover a variety of topics including nonprofit management, leadership, finance, and human resources. In addition to classes on fundraising itself, there are courses in public speaking, understanding and managing budgets, social media marketing, and more.

Chapter Recap

In this chapter, we learned how a woman saw a desperate need to reach the youth in remote Alaska villages with a message of hope and possibility. And she used her love of music to translate that message and change lives. It's also a family affair with her son working alongside her, which makes the endeavor even more meaningful.

YOUR TO-DO LIST

- It's journaling time again. Write out your fears of being in the spotlight. How will you face that challenge? I am a big believer in writing things down as a way to make them tangible and solvable. Once you take it out of your head and into the world via the written word, it becomes real and you can deal with it more effectively and proactively. It loses the power of the mouse racing around your brain in the middle of the night ratcheting up your anxiety level.
- Take a course in public speaking or sign up for Toastmasters if you want to polish your sales pitch and attract donors to your cause.
- Consider joining an association that can provide support and learning opportunities as you get up to speed on running a nonprofit and fundraising.

WINNING STRATEGIES OF FEMALE ENTREPRENEURS

"Despite what you see on covers of magazines and case studies of Harvard Business School, the actuarial data is very clear: women over 50 are twice as likely to be as successful as other entrepreneurs," Nathalie Molina Niño, CEO and founder of BRAVA Investments, told me when I interviewed her for my Next Avenue column.

Molina Niño's company invests in start-ups and supports businesses, she says, that can prove "they are creating a measurable economic benefit that puts more money in the wallets of women. If the business world actually made decisions based on what is statistically likely to yield on investment, we would only be investing in women over the age of 50."

I regularly receive emails and calls from women interested in starting businesses and looking for guidance. Generally, they're over 50. The number of businesses owned by women in the U.S. has increased 31 times between 1972 and 2018. Four out of every 10 businesses in the United States are now women owned, employing more than 9 million and generating more than $1.8 trillion in revenue, according to American Express's 2018 *State of Women-Owned Businesses* report.

Interestingly, SCORE's latest infographic on women in business, collecting data from 20,000 U.S. small-business owners, reveals that women 65+ are the largest group among all women 18 and over (28%) to start businesses out of necessity.

This does not surprise me given the ageism in the workplace. By contrast, the greatest percentage of millennial entrepreneurs (28%) start businesses because of market opportunity. The infographic also shows that women entrepreneurs across age groups (44%) are most likely to choose an industry based on prior experience/education, and that only 27% of women business owners seek outside financing.

After 50 can be a great time in life for women to launch companies. "Research shows that women's confidence at work increases with age while at the same time, their family responsibilities – especially related to child bearing and rearing – decrease," Kimberly A. Eddleston, a professor of entrepreneurship and innovation at Northeastern University, and a senior editor on the EIX Editorial Board of the Schulze School of Entrepreneurship at the University of St. Thomas in Minneapolis, which publishes the Familybusiness. org site, told me. "This makes entrepreneurship over 50 a great idea and a possibility."

Mid-Life Women and Entrepreneurial Mojo

Another compelling reason is that mid-life women have entrepreneurial mojo: "With their greater work experience and confidence, such women are more likely to see opportunities for a new business – customers whose needs are not being filled and gaps in product categories," Eddleston says. "In turn, their work experience often gives them the networks to successfully launch a business at this career stage. They also often have the financial resources to support a new business."

Sanyin Siang, author of *The Launch Book: Motivational Stories to Launch Your Idea, Business or Next Career*, told me that women have a few advantages over men as entrepreneurs. For one thing, they're often connectors. "We tend to have a diverse network," she says. "That's a diversity in terms of people with different backgrounds."

Another advantage, according to Siang: women tend to be open to "collaborative entrepreneurship." That's a terrific asset, but one that many would-be business owners dismiss.

"There is this idea that when we are starting something, we have to do it alone, to be the front and center person for it," says Siang.

In reality, she noted, "to succeed, you need to expand your thinking about what your gifts and talents are. It might not be you running that company. You might come up with the idea and partner up with someone who is much better than you at execution and implementation. That's collaboration, and something that comes naturally for many women."

David Deeds, the Schulze Professor of Entrepreneurship at the University of St. Thomas, concurs. "Entrepreneurship is a team sport, and women are good at working with others. That gives them a little advantage."

Serious Concerns for Women Entrepreneurs

We hear a lot about sexism against businesswomen and a lack of capital for women-owned enterprises. And both of these are serious concerns. Nevertheless, experts I've interviewed have consistently told me that decades of workplace experience can make a big difference in whether women's businesses thrive. "The added work experience and the associated boost to their self-confidence significantly assists in the development of their businesses," says Eddleston.

And women in mid- to late career generally have more capital of their own to invest in their businesses than younger ones. "The ability to invest more capital provides a substantial advantage to these businesses," Eddleston says.

Struggles in Year One

That doesn't mean it's easy for women owners. In the first year of owning a business, female entrepreneurs appear to struggle more than men, according to the Kauffman Foundation. Only 52% of women with first-year start-ups said their ventures performed well last year, while 67% of men said theirs did. The difference, however, fades over time. Among businesses that are five or more years old, equal percentages of men and women (77%) said their company performed well last year.

So my advice to mid-life female entrepreneurs or wannabes: stay the course.

As Maya Angelou said: "All great achievements require time."

In this section, you will read the stories of five women entrepreneurs and their journeys to follow their hearts and dreams to be their own boss.

CHAPTER 16

Health and Happiness

Ginny Corbett, Salúd Juicery
Courtesy of Michael Morgan.

For Ginny Corbett of Sewickley, Pennsylvania, it's about helping people heal. A licensed psychotherapist, Corbett was baffled that her clients (many struggling with depression and anxiety), were often relying on a catalog of pills to help combat those emotional troubles, but doing zilch to alter their routines. "They weren't thinking about what they were eating, or exercise – they were just popping a prescribed pill every day," says Corbett, who I met when I interviewed her for *Money* magazine.

So, six years ago, Corbett, now 55, began studying the gut-brain bond, learning about holistic healing of the mind, body, and spirit, and going to healthy-eating seminars. Her purpose was to learn more about "ways what someone eats can influence his or her state of mind

189

and emotional health," she says. Corbett's interest in natural eating turned her on to the health paybacks of drinking raw juice and its likely role in healing both mind and body.

The push to launch her business, a fresh cold-press juice store, was an off-the-cuff conversation with a 20-something smoothie-loving friend. It was karma. "I love being around the 20-somethings; they have so much energy," says Corbett. "One thing led to the next and before we knew it, we decided to try making some juice drinks," she says. Corbett spent $1,200 to purchase a small juicer, and the pair spent a few days in her kitchen chopping vegetables and fruits and experimenting with different recipes.

The result: Five years ago, Corbett opened the store, called Salúd Juicery (saludjuicery.com) in Sewickley, an upscale village outside of Pittsburgh, where she lives and also runs her therapy practice several hours a month.

Her customers arrived swiftly; soon more than 100 customers a day were spending an average of $9 apiece on their purchases, sending the store into the black after six months. Corbett moved quickly to open her second location across town.

The total launch cost for the first location: $90,000. Corbett tapped her savings but not retirement funds for the initial investment, which went to fix up the 1,200-square-foot space and buy inventory and supplies. The biggest outlay: $30,000 on equipment. Opening the second location cost around $120,000.

Salúd Juicery is known for its typically thick, green-tinged spinach, kale, lemon, apple, and cucumber juice mixtures, or beet-colored super-fruit smoothies blending pineapple, banana, strawberry, orange, almond, and coconut milk. But there are more than a dozen other protein-packed concoctions, including ginger and wheatgrass shots, coffee and tea-based hot drinks, and granola and muesli açai berry bowls. "Some customers see juicing as just a cool, healthy refreshment," says Corbett. "But juice fasts, or cleanses, are very popular with people who are looking to detox or diet."

The business has had a family-affair flair, with all three of Corbett's children – ages 28, 24, and 19 – habitually sampling juices, working the sales counter, or helping design marketing materials, including coaching her on how to build an Instagram following as a way to communicate with her customers and post free-beverage offers. She now has over 9,000 followers.

With an undergraduate degree in business administration, Corbett has always been fascinated by the ins and outs of running a business. She became a therapist after relocating to support a career move for her husband, a petroleum geologist and part-time pastor. But she had an entrepreneurial track record, having previously run an eclectic series of small businesses, from a maid service to an interior-design firm.

When Corbett was 23, she started her first venture, a maid service in Farmington, New Mexico. To get started, she tapped a $7,000 loan from her grandmother, which she paid back with 3% interest when she sold the business to her aunt two years later. "The business was profitable, but I hated cleaning my friend's toilets, which I had to do when someone would call in sick," she says. "I was the backup."

She also owned and operated an interior and kitchen design shop and had a hand in a small franchise business with her father and sister. "With all the businesses I have ever had, I really feel this one can go the furthest, because people continue to pay more attention to healthy eating habits," says Corbett.

Corbett has dug in. "I could have stopped at the first one and been happy that it was healing so many people," she says. "But it's like having a beautiful Ferrari in the garage; you can let it sit there, polish it and look at it, or take it out on the road and drive it and see what it can really do."

And so she felt it was her time. "This is my opus," says Corbett. "I never felt I could devote myself to a business while my kids were growing up. I didn't want to screw up my family. It doesn't matter how successful you are if you mess up on your family life."

Although Corbett loves her juices and quaffs them on a regular basis, the art of small talk or preparing a perfect juice or smoothie is not what drives her. "I enjoy talking to the customers, but the truth is I'm in my business office every day," she says. "If I'm at the store too much, I'm not doing my job – making sure we have the product and dealing with food costs and payroll. It's not just the product you need to love. You have to love running a business to have a business."

By the end of 2018, Corbett had a total of seven Salúd Juicery locations around Pittsburgh – four company stores and three licensed stores – and one in State College, near the Penn State campus. And she is adding more franchisees. Projected revenue: $2 million. Corbett currently pays herself a salary but reinvests most of the profits to fuel franchising and wholesale opportunities. She boosts her income with an additional $18,000 a year from the scaled-back therapy practice.

That said, Corbett hasn't abandoned her healing vision for the women she still counsels and others. She is also writing a book about emotional healing. "It's altruistic, but my hope is that my products will help people on their journey. That's what I really want to do."

After all, in the beginning, Corbett says, she just wanted to help people heal.

Making It Work

I asked Ginny to look back and share her thoughts on starting her chain of juice bars.

> **Kerry: What did starting your own business mean to you personally?**
>
> **Ginny:** I have thought a great deal about why I do what I do, and I always come back to the same thought: it is something that is inside of me, and I would never have been truly happy until I did it. I think starting a business is a spark that won't leave you alone until you bring it to fruition. Once it is brought to life it very much has its own personality and demands its own destiny.
>
> **Were you confident that you were doing the right thing? Any second-guessing?**
>
> I second-guess myself every day of my life, but I do not let it cause me to waver. Constantly evaluating what you are doing, why you are doing it, and where it is going is my way of not getting soft and content. It is the frog in boiling water concept. If you put a frog in hot water it will jump out, but if you put a frog in cold water and turn up the heat gradually, it will allow it and boil to death. That can happen to us in life when we accept the things we know are not what we want in the big picture. I don't ever want to lose the fire or the passion. Life is short and I want to offer my gifts and talents to make this crazy world a better place.

Anything you would have done differently?

Hindsight is magical, but I don't think it is a good thing to beat ourselves up with. Sure, I would have avoided a few things if I would have known then what I know now. But I don't regret anything. It really is about the journey, not the destination. Everything I have done has prepared me for the next level or the next venture. I believe there is a divine intervention in business just as in life. We need to meet the people we meet, and we gain and give from the experiences we have.

How do you measure your success?

I honestly don't know how to answer that. Looking to the past, which I never enjoy doing, there are some things I have already accomplished that my younger self would have considered as markers of success. I think there is an expectation of success and a drive to build that resides in my soul. There is always a bigger mountain. I have found that success in business and personal success tend to merge into the same thing as you get older. Personally, I believe I was put on this earth for a reason, and I have been uniquely equipped with the ability to fulfill my purpose. My purpose is fueled by my passion. I am passionate about coming alongside people while they emotionally heal. You will never fully know how your life and actions affect other people, and you will never know to what extent your passion changes the world.

Success is no longer checking off certain boxes but an ongoing personal gut-check with how fully I am living. It is a resolve to live passionately and fearlessly and love people well.

What books or resources did you use or recommend others to use?

Early on in my business venturing I found a book that was life changing, *The E-Myth* by Michael Gerber. It was all about how to systematize your business and be realistic about your role. And I better go back and read that book again. When my business needed to make a jump away from the "one off" mentality, I really appreciated Jim Collins's book, *From Good to Great*. But truthfully, when it comes to a guide for life, integrity, and centering myself for the grind, I turn to the wisdom and inspiration from the Bible. I enjoy Eugene Peterson's version, *The Message*.

What are some of the unexpected rewards and surprises?

I will never know if the choice I made long ago to own my urge to be an entrepreneur and open my own businesses, instead of taking the traditional career route and report for a paycheck, was a beneficial choice for my family or was net negative for them. It certainly set the tone for a way of life. Each of my children was born into a different business era. As a woman in business who has spent a lifetime trying to balance demands of my family and demands of my business, I think the biggest reward I have had in business is when my grown children have told me they were proud of me and called me a badass! There is no greater reward than that. Period.

Lessons learned?

I could not possibly reduce the lessons I have learned to paper. I am kind of kidding, but kinda not.

Biggest challenge?

I know the ideal is work to live, not live to work, but I always wonder when to quit and when to push forward. My daily challenge is summed up well with the serenity prayer as I fearlessly attempt "to change the things that I can and find serenity to accept the things I cannot." But always, my biggest challenge is finding the wisdom to know the difference.

WOMEN 50+: DECLARE YOUR INDEPENDENCE AND START A BUSINESS

One of the best decisions I ever made was to declare my freedom from my full-time job as a columnist for a national newspaper and start my own business as a freelancer. That was my personal independence day, and I've never looked back. Since then, I've also become an author of numerous books, a frequent public speaker, and an expert on jobs for people over 50.

So my question for women: Is it time for you to declare your independence and start a business?

For many women I have met and counseled, launching a business at mid-life is often an inner pursuit to find meaning and to give back to society. That's tremendously rewarding. What's more, becoming an entrepreneur after 50 is not as risky as you may think (or needn't be), and the psychic and financial payoffs can be well worth it. Plus, launching a business is one answer to both the gender pay gap and the lack of advancement many women feel in today's workplace.

You don't have to go it alone, and you needn't be afraid to seek help, though. "Many universities offer entrepreneurship assistance for alumni, several offer programs and workshops specifically geared towards women, and there are many local organizations – often government-supported or nonprofit – whose goal is to help women start and manage their own businesses," Kimberly A. Eddleston, of Northeastern University and the EIX Editorial Board, says.

I suggest you tap into the site of the U.S. Small Business Administration (SBA), SBA.gov, as well as Score.org, a nonprofit that provides small-business assistance. Both are top resources for local seminars and other types of help for newbies. The SBA's Office of Women's Business Ownership assists women entrepreneurs through programs coordinated by SBA district offices, including business training, advice on snagging federal contracts, and tips on getting access to credit and capital. It oversees Women's Business Centers (sba.gov/tools/local-assistance/wbc), a national network of over 100 educational centers.

"Do not assume that these organizations are only for high-growth businesses; many have programs for all types of businesses," Eddleston says.

I agree with all of Eddleston's suggestions and would like to offer eight more of my own:

Be clear-eyed about your prospects. Don't expect to make a substantial profit straightaway. Be content knowing that the reward, at least initially, will come from doing something you love, following a dream, and being your own boss. I call this "intangible income," and it's tax-free.

(Continued)

WOMEN 50+: DECLARE YOUR INDEPENDENCE AND START A BUSINESS *(Cont'd)*

Take it slow. Your skill set and experience offer the basis to starting your venture, but it will take time to lay the groundwork for a successful launch. You'll need to do your research to be assured there's truly a demand for your prospective service or product in the marketplace. Consider, too, which new skills you might need in order to get your business up and running. To learn them, volunteer or moonlight, if possible. Also, ask other small-business owners in your field how they got started and dealt with challenges.

Don't wreck your hobby. Be aware of the distinction between a hobby that's a remedy to your frenzied working world and a pursuit that's really something you can relish 'round the clock. I love horses, for example, but a business teaching horseback riding would be a recipe for disaster for me. Horses are my escape valve and that's the way I like it.

Consider hiring a career coach or a life coach. Personally, I've found that an unbiased outsider can help keep me motivated and focused on the next steps for keeping my business viable. This kind of advice and accountability can be invaluable when you're planning and launching your business.

Assemble a support team. Confiding in a spouse or partner, a mentor, a friend, a sibling, or even your adult child can keep you balanced and help you steadily navigate the uncharted landscape of founding a business.

Get a firm grip on your finances. Many first-time entrepreneurs overvalue their initial income and undervalue their start-up costs. Do you have enough socked away to support a few years with lower income (or none at all) if you will plow net income back into the business to keep it growing?

Be ready for obstacles. If you've laid the proper groundwork, you'll get through the bumpy bits. Having your support team to lean on will help.

Create the proper mindset. This is something Sanyin Siang, author of the excellent *Launch Book*, told me when I interviewed her for my Next Avenue column. The best approach is to begin with a vision of where you want to go, tape a picture on your office wall of what it might look like or set it as your computer's screensaver, and journal about your goals.

Get things stirring with small steps and before you know it, you'll be able to jubilantly declare your independence.

9 TIPS FOR WOMEN ENTREPRENEURS FROM THE AUTHOR OF *THE LAUNCH BOOK*

Sanyin Siang, author of the excellent book *The Launch Book: Motivational Stories to Launch Your Idea, Business or Next Career*, radiates a sense of possibility for women entrepreneurs.

After reading her book, I Interviewed Siang, 44 (who's executive director of the Fuqua/Coach K. Center on Leadership & Ethics at Duke University and has served on the board of several start-ups), to hear more on how women launching businesses at mid-life can combat what she calls "the fear of failure."

What I especially liked about *The Launch Book* is that it addresses a key factor that people hoping to run successful businesses often overlook: having the right mindset. "Whether you are a 20-year-old entrepreneur or a 70-year-old entrepreneur, what is critical is your mindset," Siang told me.

Here are nine of my favorite mindset strategies pulled from my conversation with Siang:

1. **Understand your values.** "How you discover what is important to you is a reflection of where you are spending your time and what gives you energy. We think there is something we value. Yet when we look back, and we chart where we are spending time and what energizes us, it is often something very different. So having an awareness of the alignment of the two is key. It's an anchor that has to be put into place and everything else flows from there."

2. **Be open to luck.** "When you are able to accept that luck plays a role, you are also accepting that not everything is in your control. That means that successes are not always in your control, and neither are failures. Luck has to do with timing. It has to do with the people who come into your life. And if we are so focused on the planning and a very linear path, we may be missing out on the huge opportunities that come from luck. Being able to leverage luck, or being able to be prepared for luck, means being able to have that open mind to seeing and being in the moment."

3. **Love the truth tellers and naysayers.** "I believe you have to find people who energize you. However, there are people who, every idea you have, will say, 'That won't work.' Those people we tend to dismiss, or we let their judgment hold us down. But here's how we leverage that naysaying: it is asking them 'Why do you think this won't work? Help me understand.' They might be seeing something you aren't. The key is to explore what they are seeing that may cause an obstacle in your launch, so that you can proactively address it. It is not to take their answer of "No," or "This is a terrible idea," at just that, but to go deeper."

(Continued)

9 TIPS FOR WOMEN ENTREPRENEURS FROM THE AUTHOR OF *THE LAUNCH BOOK (Cont'd)*

4. **Seek out mentors.** "Being able to reach out to someone who has gone through what you are going through is a great way to shortcut a lot of the ups and downs. It is not about mirroring their exact path, but understanding from their wisdom, the path you can take."

5. **Understand your idea's relevance.** "We can all launch things in silos, but what will give it a better chance of gaining traction and succeeding is if it is relevant. There are two ways of thinking about relevance. One way is relevance to yourself, which ties into your purpose. The other one is the relevance to the audience for what you are trying to start.

   "A key way to build relevance with your audience is at the start to co-create with your customers. Say you have an idea for starting an ice cream business. Well, there are a ton of ice cream businesses out there. Your customers need to understand what is in your story, your background. Why do you want to start this ice cream business? You need to ask potential customers what will make them want to come and get your ice cream. What will be the differentiators? What needs are not met in the market right now? If you can co-create with them, by the time your ice cream shop opens it will be relevant, and you will have that traction."

6. **Develop gumption.** "Every launch is a change, and change is uncomfortable. It requires a degree of gumption, or courage. You need to be brave. Courage isn't the absence of fear. It is not going blindly into something, but understanding what the risks are. Courage is being able to step forward because it is connected to your purpose and values and how you are going to help make a difference in the world. Thinking about courage in that way actually allows you to have the gumption to proceed."

7. **Show your vulnerability.** "This is a huge one, especially with women, who tend to struggle with the pursuit of perfection. When we try to have all of the answers, we are not allowing others to invest in our success, and we all get joy from investing in others. Vulnerability is what enables us to recognize what we are lacking. Once we recognize that, it allows us to go out and find the right mentors and the right advisers to help us navigate. And vulnerability also helps us be more relatable. That aspect of saying, 'I am creating an ice cream shop. I don't have the answer to this question. Can you help me?' That is an opening door to collaboration, to relevance, and the way to leapfrog the experience gap you have. You are also going to be able to connect with yourself and have an understanding of your strengths and your weaknesses."

---

8. **Let in the laughter.** "We all know when we are launching that we are going to go through ups and downs. Laughter energizes us. It draws the team together. If you are a solo entrepreneur, being able to look at things with a sense of humor gives you perspective. I don't think we can overestimate the power of laughter. Laughter gives us that space, that pause that then enables us to imagine. And imagination keeps you moving forward."

9. **Practice generosity.** "You need to lift others up. Resilience is a word we hear about today over and over. However, our society has been talking about resilience in an incomplete way. I think resilience is a factor of generosity. I know it is counterintuitive, but when you are down on your luck, and you are generous, it gives you a sense of perspective. It enables you to be more resilient.

"Don't think about being generous only when you have made it, but be generous from the get-go with your time and your wisdom. The act of generosity doesn't take a lot of time or effort, but it has tremendous impact on both you and the receiver."

Chapter Recap

In this chapter, we learned how a woman has built a business out of her desire to help women manage their health better for physical and mental wellness, and also learned some ways to shift our mindsets to help us launch our businesses.

YOUR TO-DO LIST

- Make a list of people who might be potential mentors.
- Do one thing today to help someone else: either share advice, a contact, or an ear for listening.
- Write down in your journal the funniest thing you saw or heard today and laugh out loud. Tell someone else what that was. It might even be something you did or happened to you. Feels good, right?

CHAPTER 17

Chilling Out

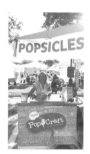

Donna Tortorice, Pop Craft

On the October day in 2009 that Donna Tortorice debuted her pushcart at the St. Petersburg Farmers Market, she sold 500 popsicles in the first two hours. She was flabbergasted.

Now, the 69-year-old founder of Sarasota, Florida–based Pop Craft (popcraftpops.com) peddles around 30,000 pops each month, and that figure is rising.

"Before I went to the farmers market that day I didn't know what to expect," Tortorice says. "I had been sampling them out to my friends and family. They all, of course, said they were great, probably because they were related to me, or wanted to encourage me."

The former catering executive spent an estimated $25,000 to launch her business, including $4,500 for her pushcart. Other costs included machinery to make the product and ingredients. And all of that was self-funded from her personal savings, not retirement accounts.

And she also got lean and mean by downsizing from a 4,000-square-foot home to one that's 1,200 square feet. She cut back on spending and put the brakes on travel. "I knew I didn't want to be in debt," she says. "It's so hard to start a business from scratch anyway, and then if you go into debt, it makes it so much more difficult. I bought things as I could afford them, and I've grown my business from the very beginning in that manner. Today, the business is debt free."

The pops, which are modeled after Mexican ice pops, or *paletas*, change hands for anywhere between $4 and $6 each. Today, she owns two pushcarts that wheel around the farmers markets in Sarasota and St. Petersburg, and one that's reserved for special event rentals. Plus, she has a solo franchisee, a wholesale account, who operates a food truck in Sarasota that sells her pops.

The bulk of Pop Craft's sales, though, come across the counter at her retail store, via wholesale accounts (the biggest chunk of her business) with regional vendors like Disney, Marriott, and Ritz-Carlton, and through online sales of boxes of pops, which retail for $37.50 to $49.50 per box of 10 to consumers nationwide. She also regularly caters special events and parties. "I remember when I thought selling 1,000 pops a week was amazing – it wasn't that long ago," she says.

It wasn't until she opened her bricks-and-mortar shop that Tortorice truly comprehended that her pops were hot. "I thought I would have people walking in who would buy one popsicle, maybe two popsicles, if it was a couple. But I had boxes of pops in a freezer, and customers began to buy boxes, and building their own box with a variety of 10 pops. "It's hard to believe, but I now have customers who will spend up to $200 a month on boxes of *popsicles*."

Annual popsicle sales are now close to $1 million, and she's in the black and pays herself. That said, "I've been putting money back into the business from the beginning to keep it growing," she says. "And I employ, depending upon the time of the year, anywhere from six to nine associates to handle production, run the shop, and operate pushcarts."

Her frozen delicacies include ices and creams, such as a caramel sea-salt pop. Their appeal? Quirky flavors like blueberry lemon basil, white chocolate mint pistachio, and all-natural peanut butter dipped in dark chocolate and dusted with gray sea salt. In total, she has 50 different recipes, which she rotates. Her bestseller: Mexican chocolate, a mixture of Belgian chocolate with a touch of sweet cinnamon.

And there's a healthy angle to her offerings. The gourmet pops contain no corn syrup, artificial ingredients, preservatives, or additives. And they're made with whole fresh fruits, vegetables, and herbs. There are also vegan, gluten-free, sugar-free, and dairy-free options.

Pop Craft's flavors turn seasonally, as Tortorice works to keep ingredients as local as possible. She uses Florida citrus, such as mangoes from Sarasota orchards.

When One Door Closes

Tortorice's desire to launch her own business was spurred after she lost her job in 2006 as director of catering at Morton's Gourmet Market and Catering in Sarasota. After a 30-year career in the food and beverage business with employers such as The Colony Beach and Tennis Resort in Longboat Key and the Hyatt Regency Sarasota, finding a new position was tougher than she ever imagined. "At my age, 57, it was kind of hard to get rehired, to be honest with you," says Tortorice. "After a certain age, employers don't want all that experience. What I thought was an asset didn't work for me."

It took three years of job hunting and soul-searching, but like many older entrepreneurs, Tortorice grew fed up with rejection, and harkened back to her childhood for inspiration. Her love of icy treats traces to her New England upbringing in Old Lyme, Connecticut. "The Good Humor man was the thing when I was a little girl," she says. "We lived on the shoreline in New England. The Good Humor man was at the McCook's Point Beach overlooking Niantic Bay all the time, and I loved those popsicles."

Then too, Tortorice comes from a large Italian family. "My dad was all about sweets and lemon ice," she recalls. "Food was big. We would spend one day talking about what we were going to make, then we would make it the next day, then we would eat it, and then we would be talking about what we were going to make the next day. It never stopped."

Food was inextricably part of her DNA. In fact, back in the 1970s, she trained to be a chef, after attending a business college, and she worked in several commercial kitchens. She also ran a cooking school. But when she moved to Florida in 1979, she couldn't land a job working in a kitchen. "Commercial kitchens weren't hiring many females back in those days, unless you wanted to work in the salad department," she says. So she transitioned to work in sales and marketing.

Family Ties

She credits her son, Martin Scott, now 44 and a sommelier in Atlanta, with helping her come up with the idea. He had sampled a gourmet artisanal popsicle in Georgia and called to tell her that he thought this kind of foodie item was going to be big. He urged her to try making and selling the treats in Florida. She had nothing to lose. And she loved playing around in the kitchen. So Tortorice started doing some research, creating recipes with Scott's input, and making popsicles in her kitchen.

"I feel like I'm an artist," she says. "I'm always creating, coming up with ideas, forming the plans, and carrying it out, trying to make everything successful. I think that's probably what every entrepreneur has inside them. For me, that's the part that I thrive on. Every single day I look forward to coming into work and doing what I'm doing. It makes all the difference in the world."

Making It Work

I asked Donna to look back and share her thoughts on starting a popsicle business.

> **Kerry:** *What do you tell other people who ask for your advice?*
>
> Donna: When you run your own business, there are ups and downs along the way and you can make mistakes, but you just have to pick yourself up and move on and not get discouraged. Importantly, pay close attention to funding. You can't start underfunded. I started small, and I was educated in what I was doing – the food business. Don't start something you don't know anything about because it is too difficult.

Lessons learned?

After the success of my own pushcart, I bought a few more. Then I started selling small pushcart franchise operations to other people who wanted to make extra money on the weekend, or people like myself who were unemployed and wanted to do something. It wasn't a huge investment,

Soon we had eight pushcarts operating in Sarasota, St. Petersburg, Tampa, and Orlando. It was the wrong direction, though, and set me back a bit.

I lost some money mostly because of the amount of my time it took up. It was very complicated with all these different people out there selling the pops, and it was very hard to monitor what each one was doing and the quality. I realized then what franchising was all about and why there are so many guidelines.

Ultimately, it turned into a positive thing. It helped to get product brand recognition and from that point it grew to a wholesale business.

Biggest challenge?

Hitting the brakes. I have to pull myself in once in a while. I'm always 10 steps ahead of myself. I have so many ideas. Sometimes I have to say, okay, we're working on this now. I'm always wanting to develop and go forward. In the middle of the night, I'm thinking … we can do this; we can do that.

Biggest reward?

Smiling customers. The satisfaction of seeing all my dreams and my thoughts coming true and how it translates into people being happy. When someone eats a popsicle, they smile.

8 WAYS WOMEN ENTREPRENEURS CAN USE CROWDFUNDING SUCCESSFULLY

It takes money to make money, as the saying goes. For female entrepreneurs, that money can be elusive when starting a business or trying to grow one. As Linda Abraham – a serial entrepreneur, angel investor, and start-up board member – told me when I asked her to name the biggest hurdle for female entrepreneurs: "Raising capital. I am sorry to say that, but it's true."

I've interviewed several women in the early stages of starting ventures and each said that having enough seed money in the bank is what's slowing them down. A few said they've considered launching a crowdfunding campaign – raising cash online through a campaign inviting people to help you. But they were nervous about taking that nontraditional lending route.

Crowdfunding can actually be a very effective way to get a business off the ground and keep it rolling. And women are increasingly taking advantage of it. These days, 47% of successful campaigns on the popular crowdfunding site Indiegogo are run by women, according to Sarah Meister, the site's outreach manager.

There are also a few crowdfunding platforms specifically for women entrepreneurs, such as iFundWomen (ifundwomen.com) and Women You Should Fund (womenyoushouldfund.com). Local cohorts of iFundWomen have been launched in Boston, Nashville, Newark, Philadelphia, and Raleigh-Durham, as well as the state of Maryland.

Last November, New York City launched a program to lend women business owners money through a crowdfunding site called We Fund: Crowd (we.nyc/we-fund-crowd/). The premise: Lend a woman at least $25, and after she pays it back, you can then lend it to another woman's business plan or simply put it back in your pocket.

To address the concerns of women entrepreneurs over 50 (or women that age hoping to start businesses) who are jittery about using crowdfunding, I spoke to three experts on how to create winning campaigns. One was Meister; the second was Jen Earle, CEO of the National Association of Women Business Owners (NAWBO.org) and council member of the National Women's Business Council (NWBC.gov), a nonpartisan federal group that advises the president, Congress, and the U.S. Small Business Administration on economic issues important to women business owners. The third was Donna M. De Carolis, dean of the Charles D. Close School of Entrepreneurship at Drexel University and a member of the editorial board of EIX (eix.org), the Entrepreneurial and Innovation Exchange, a social media learning platform funded by the Schulze Family Foundation.

Over recent years, women have become very active on crowdfunding platforms, according to Earle. In fact, recent data on Kickstarter shows that on average, they are 9% more successful than men. One reason is that women usually set lower funding goals than men. The average funding goal for men was much higher, but the average amount pledged was about the same.

Some types of businesses are better bets for successful crowdfunding campaigns than others. Says De Carolis: "Overall, crowdfunding is more appropriate if you have a gadget to sell or are a local small business. Food products, fashion, and nonprofits in some cases tend to have success with crowdfunding."

Here are the three experts' eight tips for crowdfunding wisely:

1. **Be sure you have a following.** "Before you jump into a crowdfunding campaign, you need to have a cadre of people who will recognize you as having legitimacy or expertise in an area," De Carolis says. "A social media presence with a lot of followers can do a lot to legitimize your product and make you legitimate in a crowdfunding space ... At the end of the day, even with venture capital funders, 99% are investing in the person, not the business."

2. **Tell your story well.** Here's where women can "have an edge," says De Carolis. "This is a platform to pour your heart out and talk about your product and your story and get to the emotion. In my view, that contributes to the power of women in crowdfunding. Women bring authenticity, transparency, our connection with emotion. We can tell a story about our product or gadget that can be more powerful."

   Meister agrees: Women are successful crowdfunders because they're great storytellers and great marketers. They're better at writing and talking with less dry language [than men] and they often have the altruistic component ... Having that panache and the willingness to be your true self is why women have been so successful on this platform."

3. **Know your audience.** According to Meister, entrepreneurs with successful campaigns often start a year before launch, building and testing their audience, making sure their content is resonating with their customers, so when they launch they are not just putting something out into the ether without really feeling it out.

   Your email list is going to be your best friend. In general, you can plan on converting 1% to 5% of your email list to donors to your crowdfunding campaign.

4. **Figure out a realistic crowdfunding goal and timetable.** Create a budget spreadsheet and list the basic expenses you will encounter in launching your business, including anticipated taxes and fees. Find other similar businesses and projects that have crowdfunding campaigns and note how much they had as their goals. A one-month campaign is generally best, according to Meister.

(Continued)

8 WAYS WOMEN ENTREPRENEURS CAN USE CROWDFUNDING SUCCESSFULLY *(Cont'd)*

5. **Decide on a crowdfunding model.** Women entrepreneurs, at any age range and in any industry, must evaluate the type of crowdfunding platform that is best for them. The findings in the NWBC March 2018 *Crowdfunding as a Capital Source for Women Entrepreneurs* reports, *Kickstarter, a Reward-Based Crowdfunding Platform*, and *Kiva, a Non-profit Lending Crowdfunding Platform*, as well as previous research, show that there are fundamental differences in crowdfunding platforms. Review the different platforms based on your campaign goals.

   Some platforms focus purely on donations and no one expects a return on their investment. Others offer rewards for donations, such as free products from the company. Still other crowdfunding campaigns offer a small percentage-ownership equity stake or royalties on sales. Finally, there's peer-to-peer lending, where you pay back the amount loaned to you interest free.

   Lending- and equity-based platforms seem more suitable for established businesses raising money to grow, according to the NWBC research.

6. **Understand the fees.** Different crowdfunding platforms have different fee structures and you'll want to understand the charges before launching a campaign.

   Funding on Kickstarter, for example, is all-or-nothing. No one is charged for a pledge toward a project unless the project reaches its funding goal. If a project is successfully funded, Kickstarter charges a 5% fee to the funds collected, plus payment processing fees (roughly 3%–5%).

   Indiegogo's platform fee on all funds raised is 5%. Fees are deducted from the funds you actually raise (not the goal you set). Indiegogo also charges a processing fee of 3% plus $0.30 per transaction.

   ifundWomen takes a 5% fee on the funds you raise, "but you can feel good about that, because we pay forward 20% of our profits from standard fees directly into live campaigns on the site," according the website. In addition, credit card processors charge approximately 2.9% plus $0.30 per transaction on this site.

7. **Get professional help.** That's because "how your crowdfunding page looks, how you tell your story and continually communicate on the page is essential," says De Carolis. "You don't want to put up a sloppy site … It's a PR campaign as much as a fundraising one."

   Generally speaking, you need a video of 2½ minutes or less. "And I wouldn't take it with your iPhone," advises De Carolis. You can pay ifundWomen, for example, around $1,800 to put together a pitch video.

8. **Don't count on crowdfunding as your only way to raise funds.** Says De Carolis: "It's a mistake to think, 'I am going to crowdfund and then I am going to be able to have all I need to move my venture forward.' Quite honestly, at early stages, you need to use lots of other tools. You need to have family and friends investing. You need to have angel investors. And you need credit cards. Entrepreneurs put a lot on credit cards, and that is not necessarily a bad thing, if you go about it strategically.

Chapter Recap

In this chapter, we learned how a woman built a business out of her frustration with the ageism she faced in the job market, her passion for food, and her past experience as a cook and a food marketer. You also learned ways to find extra capital through the smart use of crowdfunding.

YOUR TO-DO LIST

- Write a list in your journal of jobs you have had throughout your life, even as a kid. What connects them? Is there a theme? Is there a career path you had to pivot from in order to make a living?
- Determine how much seed capital you have available to start a venture.
- Consider whether crowdfunding is a viable path for you to raise cash.
- Take a crack at writing a draft of "your story" in your journal.

CHAPTER 18

Design from Within

Linda LaMagna, 341 Interior Design
Courtesy of Faye Sevel Photography.

Linda LaMagna, 54, of Fort Mill, South Carolina, had said she was going to retire when she was 50. "I always added, when I say *retire* that doesn't mean I'm going to sit home and eat bonbons, but go on to the next phase of my life," LaMagna, who is single, says. But as the milestone began to approach, "I started to laugh. What was I thinking? That was a joke," says the owner of 341 Interior Design (341interiordesign.com).

For more than 25 years, LaMagna's career had been a whirlwind trajectory, with stretches of living overseas in Germany and the Netherlands. She was vice president of global marketing and strategic planning for Spiracur, a medical device start-up founded out of the Stanford BioDesign Innovation Program. She worked in a variety of senior management positions for ConvaTec, a $2 billion medical device company, including being the general manager for all German-speaking markets.

"I have lived and worked all over the world and loved it," LaMagna says. "It really was my passion to be in the corporate world working on the sales and marketing side."

Her final corporate post: senior vice president of sales and marketing for the wound care/vascular division of BSN Medical, where she ran all the sales and marketing activities for the lymphology, wound care, and phlebology therapeutic markets, based out of Charlotte, North Carolina. She landed there in 2014.

By then, LaMagna's special birthday was looming. "I realized I had moved to Charlotte, and it was the first time in about 10 moves where I had chosen the location," she says. "It was finally about me. But I realized, I was *not* having fun. My work was no longer a joy to me."

It was time – time to *retire*. "One night in December of 2015 I woke up in the middle of the night just tormented by my job," she says. "I started to think: Where can I go? I have to go. The idea of putting on the blue suit and going to interview for the same job that I already had didn't thrill me."

She also realized that she was not willing to relocate again. "In the past, I was always willing to pick up and move to where the next big job was," LaMagna says.

It was more than the job though. There was something about that 50th-birthday promise she had made to herself (and boldly told others) that was a fleeting four months way. That's what really had her sleepless. "I lay in bed that night and kept thinking what am I going to do, what am I going to do. Then, I changed the question: What do I *want* to do?" she recalls.

And it occurred to her: she wanted to do interior design. LaMagna began to dig around in her mind: "Who do I know who can help me do that? What resources do I have? What skill sets do I have? I lay there that night and began to develop a plan."

After a while, LaMagna turned over and looked at the clock, and it was 3:41 in the morning – hence the name of her interior design company.

For the next four months, while she was still at her corporate job, LaMagna enrolled in two interior design night classes at a local college to see if this was something she would like. "It was fun, and

I realized there was a lot more to it than just color and decorating a home," she says.

In April 2016, she quit her job. She was 50. Three weeks later, she turned 51. "I hit that goal of retiring when I was 50," she says with a laugh. "I realized then, though, if I really wanted to do this I had to figure out a way to gain credibility in this industry."

LaMagna enrolled in an online program that consisted of 12 courses – everything from colors and textiles to using software to build rooms. "It was a very full curriculum. I was no longer employed, but used to working eight hours a day, so I took it on as a job," she says. "I studied and researched and drew things and read books and studied hard." In three months, she was awarded a diploma in interior design from the Interior Design Institute (theinteriordesigninstitute.com).

She reached out to her neighbors. LaMagna had recently moved into her Fort Mill home. "It was a brand-new neighborhood, so we were all kind of in the same boat," she says. "Everyone was decorating these new homes. I talked to one of my neighbors about my new business, and she said she'd like some help with design and decorating, and I said great. I will not charge you for my time." And so it began.

So what does a background in sales and marketing in the medical device industry have to do with a starting an interior design business? "It wasn't like I repainted my bedroom and rearranged the furniture all the time when I was a kid," LaMagna says. "It came out of the work I did professionally. I was a marketer and had to understand what the customer was thinking and what their needs were and translate that into an advertisement that looks appealing."

And the fact that she had lived all over the world and moved multiple times required her to continually reconfigure furniture and make it all fit in multiple living spaces, from apartments to houses. "I always found the process challenging," she says.

As her decorating business began to grow through word-of-mouth referrals, LaMagna started spending time at Celedore Fine Wallpapers (celedorewallpaper.com), a Charlotte boutique owned by Elayne Langley located about 20 minutes from her home. "We had so much in common," LaMagna says. "We had both come from the business world. She was in sales, and I had been in sales and marketing. She had retired ten years earlier, and had been doing interior design ever since."

The budding friendship took a turn: Langley asked LaMagna if she'd like to come and help out at the store to meet potential customers and learn more about the business. "I loved it. After six months, I invested about $20,000, and we became equal partners," says LaMagna."

The store is now a boutique design center selling wallpaper, fabric, and paint. Plus, the duo does design work for retail clients, who come into the store, and with the trade, or other designers, who visit with their clients.

The beauty of their business model: the pair carry no inventory. There are wallpaper and fabric sample books and paint samples only. When a customer places an order, she pays in advance, and the women have it shipped either to the store or directly to the buyer.

For LaMagna, the business partnership complements her own interior design practice. "It's extremely nice to have someone to bounce design ideas off. And on the business side, I don't have to take all the risks. For me, it has been kind of a safety net."

Making It Work

I asked Linda to look back and share her thoughts on starting an interior design business.

Kerry: What did the transition mean to you personally?

Linda: It was something that I had a passion for, and I would have fun doing. That's it – getting back to having fun. I used to have fun in my 20s and 30s and early 40s. This was a chance to do something that was that for me again.

It reduced my stress level, but challenged me as well. That has always been important to me. Every job I have taken has been about some area of growth for me. For me personally, it also got me out of my comfort zone to do something that was completely new and to build entirely new networks.

Were you confident that you were doing the right thing? Any second-guessing?

Never second-guess. There were things I thought I would enjoy about interior design that I realized I don't. Other things that I never thought of, that I really enjoy doing. Certainly there was an evolution and a learning process in what interior design meant to me and how I was going to pursue it.

For example, having the store is really big for me. I like the idea of being more structured. And it turns out, spending a lot of time in stranger's houses doesn't really appeal to me.

Anything you would have done differently?

No. Part of that answer is how I have lived my life. I believe that you have to take chances, and you have to just dive in. I have done that a number of times. When you pick up your life at 40 and move to a foreign country by yourself, that's diving in. When you decide to start a whole new career at the age of 51, that's diving in.

In my career, there has always been a plan, a dream, or a goal, but there has always been flexibility in such a way that I have never regretted anything. You have to do it. You have to try it.

In the back of my head, there is always the thought – what's the worst that can happen? For me, if I tried and failed, or tried it and hated it, I could always go back to the corporate world. That was my safety net.

How do you measure your success?

For me, success is measured by, do I believe I am good at what I do? Am I growing as a result of that? That is my first measurement.

How big a role did financial rewards play in your decision to make a transition?

I didn't need to have a financial goal because part of my plan for 30 years and saying I was going to retire at 50 was the ability to not need to have an income at this stage of my life.

Having said that, it is so much fun to watch the growth of the store and to take that tiny nugget of gold that Elayne started and grow over the past three years has been immensely fun.

How did your preparation help you succeed?

I was fortunate to have a career coach to work with as I was making the transition. Much of the work we did was understanding, what am I carrying with me through my experiences that is beneficial and supportive of this new set of skills that I want to do? How do I actually make that transition to change corporate speak to design speak?

How do I introduce myself differently now that I'm not in the corporate world? Often someone's identity is tied to what they have done for so long, so to start something new has all those challenges with the new career, new role, new skill set, but it is also shifting your identity. How do you position yourself so that the first time you walk through the door into a cocktail party and someone asks, "What do you do?"

What do you tell other people who ask for your advice?

The first thing I say is build credibility for no one else but yourself. Whatever that means to you. Build a network and talk to people about what the business you want to start is. If I had walked into Elayne's store, bought wallpaper, and walked out without talking about my story – I am new to this and this is why I want to do it – we would never have become partners. So talk to people out there. There are people who want to help you and to help you build your network as well. I am a big believer in putting things out there. If you are starting to believe you can do this and you start putting it out there in the world, it will come back to you.

What books or resources did you use or recommend others to use?

My biggest resource was my career coach. When she called me, I said I have no use for you, I'm getting out of the corporate world. She urged me to meet with her once. That led to many more sessions where she challenged me in terms of what do you need in order to believe that you can do this? What resources do you need to build, and how do we put together that elevator speech about who you are? There were so many areas, but one of them was, "How do your Mondays look and how will they?"

For me, Monday morning was about getting up and hitting the road and going. They are very different now. I have learned it was about changing what I do, but also about changing who I am. My everyday life changed dramatically. I worked six days a week. I traveled constantly. I never had a free moment. I thought the higher up the ladder I got, the more freedom I would have. The higher up I got, it was worse.

What are some of the unexpected rewards and surprises?

One of them is that this change has allowed me to build a very different life than what I had. I have time to do many of the sub-goals I wanted. I said I wanted a dog. But you don't get a dog when you travel five days a week and you work 80 hours a week. I wanted to be able to work out and focus on my health and my body much more. So the one change that really had a trickle-down effect that led to many more positive changes in my life: Maximillian. He's a Maltese. He comes to the shop every day and greets everybody who walks in. I have this partner in crime.

Lessons learned?

You will probably work as hard or harder building your own business as you did working for somebody else, at least initially. It is scary at first. You are so far out of your comfort zone in terms of who you are and what you do and whether or not you think you can profit.

I knew my financial advisers said you don't have to worry about money, but it was a very odd feeling to not collect a paycheck when I quit to start my new business. It took a solid year and a half before I understood my financial position. I *had* saved adequately. That was a real hurdle I had to get over, and it wasn't easy. Today, my design business is growing and sales at the design center have more than doubled each year. We expect revenue to easily exceed $750,000 in 2018.

MOIRA ALLAN'S BEST MOVES FOR ENTREPRENEURIAL SUCCESS

To get a global perspective of the growing cadre of mid-life entrepreneurs, I asked Moira Allan – the cofounder and international coordinator of the Pass It On Network (passitonnetwork.org), an internet peer-learning platform that connects positive aging advocates from around the world so they can share their strengths to help each other, their communities, and themselves – to share some of her advice.

I first met Allan, who lives outside of Paris, when I was attending an Encore.org conference at the beautiful Cavallo Point: The Lodge at the Golden Gate in Sausalito, California, where we sat on the front porch and chatted about a range of issues concerning work and aging. I was charmed and impressed by her energy and global vision. I know you will be, too.

A bit more on Allan's background before we get to her tips. She founded 2Young2Retire–Europe. She serves on the councils of EURAG, Europe's oldest federation of senior organizations, and the International Longevity Center–France, and is the international liaison for Old'Up, the cutting-edge French association leading the way for those 70+. Her background is in journalism, public relations, management, and coaching. She is also associate director, global resources, for WK Wilton & Associates, a South Africa–based company serving international companies working in South Africa and Africa.

Here are Moira Allan's seven steps to starting a business for mid-life entrepreneurs.

1. **Nurture a clear vision** of who you really are and what you love to do.

2. **Understand how it can serve.** The choice is limitless: your neighbors, a child who needs mentoring, climate change, isolation, ageism,

digitalization ... Find out how you can best serve yourself, your community, and your society.

3. **Accept that you are responsible for your choices and that your day-to-day choices will shape your future.**

4. **Build a team, and find a mentor.** I am blessed to have Jan Hively, PhD, as my mentor, friend, and cofounder of our global Pass It On Network community. Don't go it alone.

5. **Be alive to what's happening around you – keep learning.** You can learn anything on the net at little or no cost. Read, watch videos, but whatever you do, keep learning.

6. **Find a course, preferably interacting with others in similar situations to yours, either virtually or in real life.**

7. **Forget about perfection.** ACT – idea, try it, evaluate, refine, try again. I fully believe in this French proverb: the courage to start is the primary investment in any endeavor.

What Are the Rewards of Entrepreneurship at This Stage of Life?

Global connectivity, relationships, future thinking, and stimulation. We're living the most extraordinary time in history. Everything is destructuring and restructuring at an incredible pace. A top-to-bottom overhaul of society is in full swing to accommodate the morphing of the traditional age pyramid to a third-third-third series of demographic columns, and this is happening right now, alongside the mega issues of our time. We're in a global and exponential spiral. It's certainly heady, but who would miss it? There's satisfaction in staying abreast, playing a role, and making a contribution.

And Are You Seeing an Uptick in Entrepreneurship Over 50? Where and Why?

Definitely. There's been a huge difference in attitudes since 2000. The force of numbers and economic realities are major factors. Minds are stretching. The World Health Organization (WHO) says stop thinking chronologically, think functionally. The 100-year life concept is making inroads, charting a new map of aging. Like a product, there are the early adopters, but we're moving to a tipping point on aging for so many reasons. A very encouraging emerging trend is toward "longevity planning" as opposed to "retirement planning."

GLOBAL RESOURCES ALLAN RECOMMENDS

- Encore.org: All of Marc Freedman's books and all of Kerry Hannon's works
- *The 100-Year Life*, Lynda Gratton and Andrew Scott
- Warehouse of Opportunities: warehouseofopportunities.eu
- The Future of Work Academy: thefutureofworkacademy.com
- Elizabeth Isele's Global Institute for Experienced Entrepreneurship: experieneurship.com
- Dan Sullivan's podcasts: strategiccoach.com
- Peter Diamandis's videos and podcasts: diamandis.com
- Ray Kurzweil: kurzweilai.net
- Peter du Toit, Future WorkIQ: linkedin.com/in/peterdutoit
- 50 Plus Skills: 50plus-skills.co.za
- Seoul50Plus Foundation: seoul50plus.kr
- World U3A: worldu3a.org
- U3A Online: u3aonline.org.au
- Old School House: oldschool.info/
- Global club for senior travel: thefreebirdclub.com

Chapter Recap

In this chapter, we learned how "retiring" to your own business at 50 is a dream worth pursuing. It takes planning, saving, adding skills, and partnering up to make the shift, but it's fun, scary, and richly rewarding.

YOUR TO-DO LIST

- Seek out a career coach who can help you make the transition from the corporate world to being your own boss, and who will push you to ask the hard internal questions.
- Write down what your "Monday" looks like now and what you want it to look like. Have some fun and sketch it out as a drawing, or create a "now and then" vision board.
- Explore by journaling and soul-searching how you can best serve yourself, your community, and your society.

CHAPTER 19

Nutty for Opera

Rachel Roth, OperaNuts
Photo credit: Yuling Designs.

For a couple of years, when she was growing up in Hibbing, Minnesota, Rachel Roth sold more Girl Scout cookies than anyone in her town. "I always sold more than any other kid, even when it was high school yearbooks," she recalls.

That's not surprising when you meet her. The single founder of New York City–based OperaNuts (operanuts.com) is a born sales siren.

I had my first handful of OperaNuts three years ago, when a friend of our family's, Eileen Roach, brought them as a house present to my sister and her husband's lake house in South Carolina. I was hooked. So when I had the chance to meet Roth, the creator of these mouth-watering morsels, on a trip to New York, I leapt at it.

She didn't disappoint. As I munched the samples that she had brought along in a gift bag, she regaled me with tales of her start-up, mostly how she enthusiastically reached out for help from those decades younger than her. That resonated with me.

Roth, who "is over 65, but under 100," she says, and Roach, 28, first met at a New York Public Library branch on the Upper East Side where Roach was volunteering through New York Cares (newyorkcares.org). Roach's project involved assisting older adults with their computer literacy skills on Thursday nights. The two of them hit it off. Roach quickly became Roth's techie mentor and friend. She helped Roth with a wide range of Web-related issues linked to running her budding nut business.

Roth had launched OperaNuts in 2013 with an initial investment of around $4,000 (mostly used to purchase ingredients, supplies, and packaging). Aside from the cash outlay, she conscientiously tapped into free assistance, like Roach's expertise, for extra nitty-gritty help with the mechanics of running an e-commerce endeavor.

"People in their 20s, like Eileen, have sustained me by giving me energy to keep on going," Roth says. "She helped me start my website and ramp up marketing via Mailchimp. And there are others like her who have stepped up to help me. Loraine Enchnard, for example, redesigned the website and has been with me for over a year. It continues on, and they have become dear friends. I have an imaginary charm bracelet and all of these people are on my bracelet. I call them Techies from Heaven."

Roth has been doling out homemade nuts, made with almonds, a top-secret sea salt sauce, and dark chocolate, as gifts for years. At last, she decided, after urging from friends, that she had something special to sell. "Frankly, I had to make some money," she says. And she was itching to do something beside the English language tutoring she was doing as a volunteer.

When she started testing the market, selling them at an art opening in Manhattan's Chelsea district and at the Williams-Sonoma on 59th Street, she knew she had a spot-on consumer product. "They were a hit." She called them "OperaNuts," in honor of the passion for the opera she has had since she was 12.

Her love of food, combined with her career experience, smoothed the way. Roth had a long-lasting corporate marketing career in the fashion industry at firms such as Liz Claiborne and Ellen Tracy. And she also worked as a fashion journalist. "I had marketing background, and I did a lot of research to be certain that there wasn't anything like *my* nuts in the market," she says. "But I honestly didn't have the technical skills to set up a website and learn to market online. That's where Eileen came in to tutor me."

As needed, Roth also taps other professionals for their help in other arenas. OperaNuts photographer Melissa Cruz works at Manhattan's Museum of Modern Art. Actress and model Kim Lockett came on board after meeting Rachel at the Javits Center during a trade show. She lent a hand as a retail associate at events, such as Williams-Sonoma expos. Graphic designer and artist Linda Florio works from a studio in Manhattan and joined the team after meeting Rachel in a Chelsea Market wine bar. Their shared love of culture and good food created an instant connection, and Linda consequently designed the updated OperaNuts logo.

Roth also found gratis help at Senior Planet (seniorplanet.org), a unit of the nonprofit Older Adults Technology Services in Chelsea, whose aim is to assist people 60+ become conversant with computers and the ins and outs of navigating online.

Senior Planet offers the 10-week Startup! Course, which runs for 90 minutes twice a week. Roth did not take the course, but it does sound interesting. Students learn ways to sell their products and services online, and how to create social media accounts to promote their businesses. So far, more than 50 people have taken the course. Twice a year, Senior Planet also holds a fair where its entrepreneur students can peddle their products; most of them have craft-oriented businesses.

The OperaNuts business is gaining traction steadily. Roth says her start-up is turning a profit, and she has shipped her nuts to 40 states, as well as France, Spain, Denmark, the U.K., and Australia. The nuts are now sought after for wedding favors, too, where orders of 250 bags are the norm. "That's a clientele I hadn't thought of before," she says. "But word-of-mouth marketing has created a buzz."

Making It Work

I asked Rachel to look back and share her thoughts on starting a nut business.

Kerry: What did the transition mean to you personally?

Rachel: It meant that I could follow my heart. And I have a whole new group of people and set of energies surrounding me.

Were you confident that you were doing the right thing? Any second-guessing?

The reason I was confident was because I did a lot of research, and there was nothing like this on the market. I researched the product category, price points. I wasn't going to have another cupcake business. I wanted to fill a need, and OperaNuts, the Healthy Gourmet Snack, was/is it.

Anything you would have done differently?

I would have been more tech-savvy. I wish I had paid more attention to that at the start. But I am such a people person that I think that has compensated for that. I know how to ask for help. Sometimes I wish I had a partner, somebody to bounce ideas off of, but I have Eileen and my 20-somethings, and I talk to myself a lot on the street.

How do you measure your success?

I measure my success in terms of numbers, and they are going *up*.

How big a role did financial rewards play in your decision to make a transition?

Not a lot. I wanted to make money, but I had inherited a small amount of money and had savings, so I was getting by okay. I mostly wanted something creative to do and to be out in the world and active.

How did your preparation help you succeed?

I did my research and started small in my home kitchen before expanding to a commercial one nearby. Importantly, I always have my nuts with me to share and my business card with pictures of the nuts and my website information. I spread the word one person at a time.

What do you tell other people who ask for your advice?

If you have the enthusiasm and have experience, you don't need to go to school to be an entrepreneur or study computers. Where's your passion? Are you willing to give something up? You have to. You have to stay home and take care of your "kid" – that's what your business is. There is so much to do. I am not sure how many people will really be willing to put in that kind of time and effort. It is nut by nut for me, and I spend several hours a day baking them myself – while listening to opera, of course.

I also tell them that they can't ignore the importance of doing your research. Is there a void in the market? Is your pricing right? You have to keep on tweaking and tweaking. It has to become a part of you.

You must prove that yours is a marketable product. The right merchandise, at the right time, at the right price. Then you wait for the small miracles. A catchy name helps.

What are some of the unexpected rewards and surprises?

It's amazing that I have started to get media attention. You are here. PBS Next Avenue, *Forbes*, and Market-Watch.com have published stories about OperaNuts. It's one wonderful thing after another.

Lessons learned?

Don't underestimate yourself. Don't listen to people who say it's impossible. They think small. For every problem, there is a solution. I don't get caught up. I have an open mind, enthusiasm, and experience.

WHY FLEXIBLE WORKPLACES ARE A WIN/WIN FOR WOMEN ENTREPRENEURS

Talk about synergy: Women entrepreneurs over 50, meet your flex workers. Rachel Roth has.

Increasingly, older women starting businesses without the bankroll to hire full-time, in-house workers or to set up office space are tapping telecommuting or remote workers. And it's a win/win for the entrepreneurs and their employees.

I spoke to Sara Sutton, founder and CEO of FlexJobs (Flexjobs.com), a job search site specializing in professional telecommuting, part-time, freelance, and flexible jobs, about ways women entrepreneurs can benefit from a flexible workplace:

> Kerry: *Why are women entrepreneurs in a unique position to take advantage of a flexible workforce?*
>
> Sutton: Women entrepreneurs are often in a unique position to better understand the importance of work flexibility and to value the benefits both for themselves as well as for the people they might hire.
>
> This is even more so for women entrepreneurs who are starting a company in the second half of their lives and who likely have substantial life experience to know the very real negatives that result from inflexible, often arbitrary schedules and work guidelines that typically favor men.
>
> They have the opportunity to break the cycle, while also helping their company!
>
> *What have you learned from your experience as an entrepreneur with a flexible work staff?*
>
> As a woman entrepreneur myself, as I've gotten older I have realized more and more how important flexible work options are for myself and for my team members. Flexible options such as telecommuting, and flexible and part-time schedules, allow us to both be incredibly productive professionally and also live and manage our personal lives on a daily basis.
>
> I've hired many women at all levels of their careers and stages of their lives, and they tell me regularly how flexible work options are vital to helping them manage child raising, caregiving for elderly parents, unexpected health diagnoses like cancer or postpartum depression, and allowing them the opportunity to reenter the workforce after months or decades away.

How does employing a flex work staff help your business?

Flexible work options allow entrepreneurs to recruit and retain top-tier, highly talented women and men who may not fit into a traditional work situation but who will bring a wealth of experience, education, passion, and skill to a new company.

This talent can bring tremendous benefits in terms of productivity, effectiveness, and cost savings from being able to hire people to work remotely, on flexible schedules, or part time.

How does offering flex options for workers boost women in the workplace overall?

Women entrepreneurs supporting other women through flexible work options is an important component of reducing the gender gap in the workforce, both in terms of pay and participation.

Flexible work options are especially important for working women during motherhood years in order to help achieve better gender parity in the workforce, make women more financially secure, and help reduce the negative impact the gender pay gap has on women's retirement.

COACH FOLEY'S 5 WAYS TO REV UP YOUR BUSINESS NOW

I reached out to female entrepreneur coach Mary Foley (maryfoley.com) for some power tips. I met Foley when we did an author panel together several years ago in Washington, D.C., and was blown away by her dynamic presentation. She is a Wonder Woman, red cape and all. I'm not kidding.

"I tell women that have the passion and a plan for your business," she told me. "You work hard, put in long hours, and yet you feel like you're hardly making real progress or getting results. You want to feel like Wonder Woman, but more often than not, you wonder how to generate the revenue you really want. You have the power to change that."

1. **Be super clear on what problem you solve for whom.** People pay to have their problems solved. A common challenge for women entrepreneurs is that we see a lot of problems that we can help solve and want to help everyone. It's difficult to accept that we can't. It's hard to narrow our focus on just one big problem to solve and for whom. The bigger the problem, the more someone is willing to pay to have it solved. The more we specifically describe the type of person with this problem, the more easily we can identify him or her.

(Continued)

COACH FOLEY'S 5 WAYS TO REV UP YOUR BUSINESS NOW (*Cont'd*)

Think of your top three to five clients. What trends do you notice about who they are? Industry? Position? Age? Gender? Personality? Geography? What was the top problem they paid good money for you to solve? What additional problems do they have? Focus on finding more of these top clients. Let go of the rest.

2. **Focus on your biggest revenue producers.** Often, we have too many ideas, good ideas, about how to grow our business. We try to pursue them all and we do not get enough traction or progress in any of them. Imagine you have cleared off your desk of all piles, folders, and clutter. Now put back only those few items that matter the most right now. Feel the "ahhhh ..."?

Do the same to rev up your business. Choose no more than three products or services with the best revenue potential and put all your energies there. That will mean saying "no" or "not now" to other good, decent, well-meaning products or services. That will likely mean putting your pet projects on hold. Don't worry, you can always come back to them later.

3. **Decide on a short list of high-impact Revenue Generative Activities (RGAs).** Now that you have your short list of your best revenue producers, pick three to four specific Revenue Generative Activities (RGAs) for each that have the most impact. For example: Attending a selective networking event

   - Sending follow-up emails or social media invites to those you met at a networking event
   - Giving a problem-solving presentation
   - Having a phone call, or an in-person or virtual meeting, with a prospect
   - Writing a proposal and sending it
   - Reaching out to past or existing clients
   - Sending a client appreciation gift and asking for a referral
   - Crafting and sending your e-newsletter or promotional emails

4. **Do 3+ RGAs every single day.** Consistently doing high-impact RGAs is your business growth super power! Schedule your RGAs first and commit to doing three or more RGAs at least five days a week – even with clients and other activities. This may take 10 minutes, 30 minutes, or 3 hours, but nothing is more important for growing your business than creating the habit of hustle.

5. **Speak "prospect."** When someone decides to work with or buy from YOU over others, in part it's because they believe you truly understand their

situation. Unfortunately, too many businesspeople just dive in and start telling the person what their problem is and how to start solving it.

A simple but powerful way for prospects to believe you truly "get" what they are going through is to first ask good questions, then listen carefully to the words and phrases they use to describe their problems, challenges, and aspirations. Then incorporate these same words into your response.

Chapter Recap

In this chapter, we learned how one senior entrepreneur unabashedly reached out to those decades younger who had the skills to help her navigate the technology needed to launch her e-commerce business. Likewise, she sought out free resources, flexible workers, and low-cost ways to market her product at store samplings and with hungry writers.

YOUR TO-DO LIST

- Research free resources available in your town to help you with your business concept.
- Go meet with helpers face to face. In-person tutorials are key to learning, particularly new technology.
- Review your potential client list and begin to focus your efforts on the ones with the most upside. Learning to say no is an important skill to have when you're starting out. It saves you from spreading yourself too thin and underperforming your potential.
- Investigate how you can you use flex workers to help build your business.

CHAPTER 20

The Holistic Path

Dr. Joyce Harman, Harmany Equine Clinic

One morning this past fall, I was sitting on the floor alongside Dr. Joyce Harman, 63, in the barn at her veterinary practice, Harmany Equine (harmanyequine.com), in Flint Hill, Virginia. She was meticulously inserting acupuncture needles into my 10-year-old Labrador Retriever, Zena, to help relieve a respiratory issue. All was calm, particularly Zena, who took a deep breath and nodded off.

Harman is certified in acupuncture and chiropractic, and has completed advanced training in veterinary homeopathy, nutrition, and Western and Chinese herbal medicine. And Zena is a huge fan of hers. It struck me that Harman is the quintessential representative of the type of innovative female entrepreneurs I've been interviewing and learning from as I've researched this book.

Harman delivers a range of alternative medicine and services including nutritional counseling, fitness advice, rehabilitation advice, and treatments for all species: horses, dogs, and a few cats.

She has been at this alternative medicine game for a long time, long before these kinds of treatments became part of our vernacular. After Harman graduated from Virginia Maryland Regional College of Veterinary Medicine, with an interest in acupuncture and alternative medicine, and spent a few years working for a large equine practice, she became a certified veterinary acupuncturist in 1990, and decided to open her own practice. So she moved to Virginia and opened Harmany Equine Clinic. Four years later, she became a certified veterinary chiropractor and also completed an advanced homeopathic course for veterinarians.

Harman, however, does far more than practice holistic veterinary medicine. She has written books on saddle fitting, with editions of *The Horse's Pain Free Back and Saddle Fit Book,* for Western and English horses. She also has a booklet to help introduce people to homeopathy for horses, *The First Aid Guide to Homeopathy for Horses.* And she writes extensively in both lay and professional magazines and speaks to both groups frequently. Her goal is to help educate the equine industry about natural, holistic, and integrative medicine. She also sells a line of pasture grass seeds that produce more nutritious vegetation for horses and cows. In her spare time, she's a nature photographer (harmanyinnature.com), with her works on sale at art galleries strewn around the Virginia countryside.

While all of those efforts are entrepreneurial by nature, here's the one that caught my attention. Five years ago, Harman designed and is now selling muzzles for horses. "The muzzle allows a horse to behave normally in the pasture in terms of exercise and socialization without running the risk of over-grazing," she told me.

Talk about launching a business in a field you know well where you have a built-in clientele. The muzzle sells for around $75 to $118, depending on the size, and it's customizable, meaning you can mold it to a horse's head shape to determine how much, or how little, grass is available to a horse.

Meantime, it offers 50% more breathing room than traditional muzzles, according to Harman. Her Harmany Muzzle is also made of a medical-grade plastic with Kevlar fibers, making it much lighter than other muzzles without sacrificing durability. Bonus – it's easy to keep clean with soap and water. So there's the sales pitch.

"Horses are made to graze 20 hours a day, and rest only four hours," Harman tells me. "However, in our modern rich pastures, horses and ponies can easily become obese with only a few hours of grazing per day. This leads to serious health problems, including insulin resistance; laminitis (or founder), where the feet become severely inflamed, often leading to permanent lameness or even death; and Cushing's disease."

She saw an opportunity right in front of her eyes. "Conventional grazing muzzles often do more harm than good because they don't fit right and have proper ventilation," she says.

If you ask me, that's horse sense.

Making It Work

I asked Joyce to look back and share her thoughts on starting her businesses.

Kerry: Were you confident that you were doing the right thing? Any second-guessing?

Joyce: Once I came up with the idea, I plowed ahead without thinking.

Anything you would have done differently?

The biggest thing that I have fallen down on is the marketing. I don't know anything about marketing. I have tried to learn and need to continue to do so, given the amount of money I invested to have it produced and apply for a patent (still pending), which was roughly $150,000 – most of that self-funded.

How do you your measure success?

Eventually, I want a retirement out of it. I do feel success with when the horse magazines review it without us doing anything to market it. It is somebody else noticing.

How big a role did financial rewards play?

The real reason I started the muzzle business is that the veterinary practice, done the way I do it, does not really provide a retirement payout. The big practices with multiple employees, a truck, drugs and supplies, equipment, and real estate do provide that. They can sell it. With a small private practice out of your house like I have – all you have is a client list. All I have here is me.

So behind it was the concept of having eventually a pleasant retirement business, although I will probably never stop practicing holistic medicine in some way.

Biggest challenge?

The marketing is the biggest challenge.

What are some of the unexpected rewards and surprises?

Seeing the muzzle work. People are buying them and telling other horse people about them. The emails we have had with people who have struggled to get a muzzle that fits their horse, or have struggled because their horse's face gets rubbed raw with a muzzle. The horses are happy now wearing a muzzle. Before they had to be muzzled or put in a pen with no grass at all and couldn't go out. And they really need to go out for health reasons, to go out with buddies and eat some grass and be horses.

What do you tell others who ask your advice about starting a business?

The big thing is to think it through. Think through how you are going to finance it, which is something I didn't do all that well. Do a business plan. I had done several. Follow up and see where your business is going. The exercise of doing a business plan, everybody should do. It needs to be detailed. You need to spend the time on doing it because it really does make you think. You may not follow through with all of the things you thought you might, but it is getting a better idea of what the business should entail.

Finding partners can be a good idea. The muzzle is mine, but I sometimes wish I had gone that route. The big thing is you have got to have passion for what you are doing. Because that is what keeps you going when there is $52 out of three bank accounts. There were a lot of dark days.

What books or resources did you use or recommend others to use?

It's a really old book, but I used *Business Plans That Win $$$: Lessons from the MIT Enterprise Forum.* It's simple and asks you the pertinent questions. What do you want to be when you grow up? What is your ultimate goal for this? You can get caught in the weeds with all the business plan templates that are out there.

Women Entrepreneurs: Get Certified as a Woman-Owned Business

Getting certified as a woman-owned business takes grit and tenacity. But it can potentially help land women entrepreneurs more business opportunities and government contracts.

"It's a grueling process," says Michele Meloy Burchfield, 58, cofounder of Blume Honey Water (blumehoneywater.com), a Pittsburgh-based company, when describing getting her business certified by the nonprofit Women's Business Enterprise National Council (WBENC), the largest certifier of women-owned businesses or women's business enterprises in the U.S. "But we got through it just in time to put the logo on our label. And many companies, such as Target and Starbucks, have initiatives to work with WBENC-certified companies."

Having the certification, Meloy Burchfield says, has helped Blume Honey Water ramp up sales and open doors at retailers, and will do so in the future. Certification can also help women entrepreneurs tap resources offered by the group behind the insignia, including networking events and executive education programs.

The Payoff for Getting Certified

The effort to get certified, while difficult, could repay you in spades. "The pros are increased visibility," says Donna M. De Carolis, of Drexel University and the EIX editorial board. "Most public corporations as well as local, state, and federal government purchasing agencies have programs for allotting a certain percentage of business to women-owned companies."

The U.S. government intentionally looks for women-owned businesses to award specially designated government contracts. Since 1994, the federal government has had a statutory goal of awarding 5% of eligible prime contracting dollars to women-owned small businesses, according to the National Women's Business Council, a nonpartisan federal group that advises the president, Congress, and the U.S. Small Business Administration (SBA) on economic issues important to women business owners.

Large companies and government agencies will send out a request to submit business proposals and contracts through organizations like the National Association of Women Business Owners (NWBOC) and The Women's Business Enterprise National Council (WBENC). Then, certified companies receive an email blast about upcoming project opportunities.

Who Qualifies for Certification

So, who qualifies for women-owned certification, and how do you get the designation? In general, women-owned businesses are ones at least 51% controlled by women who are U.S. citizens. One or more women must manage the day-to-day operations, and a woman must hold the highest officer position in the business and work there full time. A woman and a man can own the company jointly, but the woman must be the majority owner and demonstrate her management and control of the company.

If you'd like to apply for certification as a woman-owned business, have patience. De Carolis says it's a "lengthy application process, which in some instances can take up to a year." The WBENC's website says its processing time is generally 90 days from the date all documentation has been received.

Another potential downside: "Some women are worried about only being seen as a woman-run business, and not being taken as seriously as a man in the same industry," De Carolis says.

I say: Get over it. There's no reason to pass up a marketplace that may have a vested interest in working with you.

Admittedly, the sheer number of types of certification can make your head twirl. They range from self-certification to state certification. De Carolis's advice: "Investigate the type of certification you seek as it relates to your business and potential customers."

4 Major Types of Women-Owned Business Certification

For the sake of simplicity, I am just going to mention four types of certification for women business owners.

The SBA offers the Women-Owned Small Business (WOSB) designation. It's the best if you're aiming to score federal contracts. The SBA's process is pretty simple, De Carolis says.

Disadvantaged Business Enterprise certification, or DBE, is a federal designation performed by the state and applies to contracts through the U.S. Department of Transportation. If federal money is involved for a Department of Transportation contract, the state must include women at a pre-determined level. This certification presumes certain groups are disadvantaged, including women, black Americans, Hispanic Americans, Native Americans, Asian-Pacific Americans, Subcontinent Asian-Pacific Americans, or other minorities.

Then there's WBENC certification, which is accepted by more than 1,000 corporations, plus many federal, state, and local government entities. WBENC is also an approved third-party certifier for the WOSB.

There are no requirements for size or length of time in business here, but you'll need to pull together a wide range of paperwork and have an in-person interview to vet your company.

"Certification is the foundation of what we do," says Pamela Prince-Eason, WBENC president and CEO. "We view certification as a catalyst for business growth and a key stepping stone for women in building a successful business. It opens doors to new business opportunities and provides access to hundreds of potential corporate and government clients, as well as a network of thousands of fellow female entrepreneurs."

NWBOC also has a national certification program. Its requirements are similar to those of the WBENC. The group provides certified businesses with a mentoring program and training opportunities.

Federal versus State Certification

In addition to private third-party certifiers like the WBENC and NW-BOC, several state and local agencies offer certification programs.

Generally speaking, if you are looking to do business in the private sector, national certificates are the route to take. But if you are aiming to do business with, say, the local medical center in your town, you might check to see if there's a city agency that certifies women-owned businesses.

Once you score the certification, broadcast the news far and wide. Showcase that you're a certified women-owned enterprise on your website and in your marketing and promotional materials.

Every little edge helps.

■ ■ ■

Why Women Entrepreneurs over 50 Hold the Aces

Consider Michele Meloy Burchfield, of Pittsburgh, who you just met. As director of national accounts for the Boston Beer Company and an executive in other roles there before that, she spent 13 years "running all over the country with a full-time nanny raising her kids," she says. It wasn't working. She hit the brakes and resigned to stay at home and focus on raising her two elementary-school-aged sons. But she couldn't stand not working outside the home. So she launched a consulting firm, the MBM Group, catering to clients such as Fiji Water, D. G. Yuengling & Son, and Sierra Nevada Brewing Company.

Starting a Beverage Company in Her 50s

Then, three years ago, Meloy Burchfield took it up another gear. With her high school and college friend Carla Frank, she cofounded Blume Honey Water, a company that makes an all-natural drink combining water and bee-friendly honeys with fruit, herbs, and spices.

"Carla and I sunk our teeth into research and worked for two years developing recipes and tasting honeys from all over the world while still working full time in our respective consulting businesses," says Meloy Burchfield.

In 2017, Blume Honey Water hit shelves in Pennsylvania, the Washington, D.C., metro area, and Colorado. It's now available in the Mid-Atlantic Division Whole Foods stores, 200-plus Giant Eagle and Market District stores, MOM's Organics, and Buehler's Markets. "I feel really confident. I have almost 30 years of experience," says Meloy Burchfield.

Interestingly, when I talked to Meloy Burchfield about her challenges as a woman starting Blume Honey Water, she was emphatic about gender not being an issue for her. "It has never even crossed my mind. My mom raised me not to think of it that way. She told me to ask: 'What do you need to do to be the best to compete and add value to your business, or who you are working for?'"

No Special Obstacles as Women Entrepreneurs

I've heard similar views repeatedly from the female entrepreneurs over 50 I've interviewed in recent months. Like Meloy Burchfield, they don't feel they're facing particular obstacles launching start-ups because they are women.

As I thought about it, it occurred to me that there was a common spine among the women I've met who are becoming entrepreneurs: they cut their teeth in male-dominated industries.

As a result, over the years, they developed thick skins. And that may be a core factor for women over 50 eyeing new ventures. "Starting your own business is not for the meek," says Meloy Burchfield.

More Capital of Their Own

And when it comes to funding their start-ups, women in mid- to late career generally have more financial capital of their own to invest in their businesses.

"Since differences in financial capital are a key reason that women-owned businesses tend to struggle more than men-owned businesses and have limited growth, the ability to invest more capital provides a substantial advantage to these businesses," EIX's Kimberly Eddleston says.

Harman, for instance, self-funded her new business. Meloy Burchfield and Frank also self-funded their Blume Honey Water research while earning income from their consulting practices. The women raised $1.8 million in initial outside investment from friends and family when they were ready to start production.

The best reward for Meloy Burchfield: "It sounds romantic, but when we watch someone taste our water and look up and say, 'Wow,' you can't stop smiling," she says. "It's like your child taking the training wheels off the bike, and you see them tooling down the road on two wheels."

Launching in a Male-Dominated Field

Destiny Burns, whom you met in Chapter 3, was quick to say there were challenges, but not because she was a woman. "I have not really encountered any specific bias or issues related to my gender or age," she told me. "I have spent my entire adult and professional life in a man's world ... first the U.S. military and then as an executive in the defense sector. Most entrepreneurs I encounter are also men. I am comfortable in male-dominated business situations. I just don't see myself as any different and that's how I conduct myself."

Her saving grace was her experience. She tapped the same skills to sell her business model to lenders that she'd used in her post-military career when she made the case why the government should award her company the business.

Paying It Forward

Another corporate refugee, Barbara Rodgers, 62, launched Nutrition Life Strategies (nutritionlifestrategies.com) three years ago in Philadelphia, following a nearly 30-year career as a securities industry executive.

"After struggling with multiple sclerosis at the end of my corporate career, I was drawn to an education and career path in holistic nutrition because of the results I experienced personally in arresting my MS symptoms by changing my diet," Rodgers says. "My goal now is to pay it forward and help others who are dealing with chronic disease."

Like Meloy Burchfield and Burns, Rodgers credits her decades of experience in the workplace for preparing her to start her business. "After nearly 30 years in the securities industry – a male dominated industry, especially when I got started in the 1980s – what I'm experiencing now is refreshing. For the most part, anyone I've met in holistic nutrition is very nurturing, supportive, and friendly."

BONUS ADVICE FOR FEMALE ENTREPRENEURS FROM TWO EXPERTS I RESPECT

Nathalie Molina Niño, CEO and founder of BRAVA Investments

Molina Niño's company invests in start-ups and supports businesses that can prove "they are creating a measurable economic benefit that puts more money in the wallets of women."

Molina Niño is on a mission to champion and grow female-owned businesses. A skilled and successful serial entrepreneur, she's especially fond of women risk takers with a vision. Here are some tips she shared with me when I interviewed her for my Next Avenue column:

1. **Become a walking sandwich board.** "So you have a burning idea or a young business. Who have you told? The answer should be: everyone. Women have really good reason to be reticent to unveil things before they are fully baked, because the level of scrutiny that we are under is measurably more significant [than for men]. Perfection is what is expected of us," she told me. "Start putting things out there and allow the collective to evolve your thinking. Don't rob yourself of the community-think that helps your idea get better."

2. **Start a diverse "Mastermind" group with six to eight women.** "There is a trick to it. You need to make a commitment," Molina Niño says. And you may need to add a person or two along the way to get the best results. For her Mastermind group, she made a nine-month commitment to one special dinner with the other women each month. "We had diversity in terms of ethnicity and industries. Go outside your comfort zone for who you bring into the group," she says.

   Be sure you have an agenda for these dinners, advises Molina Niño. At her dinners, "it is not loosey-goosey," she told me. "We go around the table, and we each have a moment to talk about how we did with our previous goals. We are meant to come up with two or three concrete things we are going to do each month. These are not big, like 'improve sales,' but instead, 'add three new customers' or some measurable goal. Then the first thing you say is how did you do."

   Periodically, members need to push back. "If something didn't work, we ask each other: 'What are you going to do that's different?' So you have that accountability," says Molina Niño.

   Accountability is imperative in the initial stages of entrepreneurship because that's a period full of unknowns, self-doubt, and in many unfortunate cases, loneliness, according to Molina Niño.

(Continued)

**BONUS ADVICE FOR FEMALE ENTREPRENEURS FROM TWO
EXPERTS I RESPECT** *(Cont'd)*

When choosing the members of your Peer Circle, writes Molina Niño, "you can't rely on serendipity to bring you a network or assume your lifelong best friend will know how to support you. Use every tool available: Facebook, LinkedIn, your school, your mosque, your neighborhood bulletin boards, your chamber of commerce – these are all places to recruit."

You might also get help from an organization or business that connects and supports women entrepreneurs. Three of Molina Niño's favorites: Dreamers // Doers (www.dreamersdoers.me/), SheWorx (www.sheworx.com/), and Black Female Founders (#BFF; www.blackfemale-founders.org/).

3. **Look for resources at your day job.** Chances are you're starting your business as a side hustle, she says. Do you have resources where you work right now – "a source ... of contacts, training, support, or clientele? Can you use it to build influence and reputation that pave the way to your new business? If your new business complements, rather than competes with, your employer's, the customers and contacts you've dealt with could be a natural marketing or distribution partner down the road."

4. **Value your work.** "It's jarring to me the damage you do to your own psychological well-being when you undervalue yourself," Molina Niño told me. "When you price yourself and your product and service in a way that values your time and contribution, there is this huge upside – more than to your bottom line, but a gain in your quality of life."

Just as in salary negotiation, however, women routinely ask for less from customers and clients than men, she pointed out. There are plenty of reasons women can fall into this trap, Molina Niño says. For example, you worry you won't find customers who can afford you or that your existing customers will leave.

5. **Take breaks.** "There is no two-week vacation when you're an entrepreneur," Molina Niño says matter-of-factly. "There are no weekends." For Molina Niño, one way to stay sane as an entrepreneur is to create daily rituals.

I agree with her. If you've read other articles or books I've written, you may know that my Labrador retriever, Zena, is my road manager. In fact, in my book *Love Your Job*, I note that everything I learned about loving my job, I learned from her. So when I read the following words Molina Niño writes in her smart book *Leapfrog: The New Revolution for Women Entrepreneurs*, I became an even bigger fan of Molina Niño's:

"There's one thing in my life that keeps me from pushing it too far: my dog, Lila. If it were just me, I probably wouldn't protect those few moments of quiet that I need every day. But she's another stakeholder, and I'm never going to fail her. She's got to have her leisurely morning walk – preferably somewhere beautiful. And so I'll always have that time to recharge my batteries.

"I need my Chow Chow," Molina Niño writes. That's a move I heartily endorse.

Fran Hauser, Start-Up Investor and Media Executive

Fran Hauser, investor and author of the fine book *The Myth of the Nice Girl: Achieving a Career You Love without Becoming a Person You Hate,* also has sage advice for women 50+ who want to start a business or have done so. To succeed, you can be pleasant and gritty; collaborative and firm; likable and competent. In other words, you don't have to quash your "niceness," Hauser says.

I spoke with Hauser, 50, to hear more from her on how older women entrepreneurs can build self-confidence, deal with conflict, and balance being nice and being strong in their working lives. Here are four of my favorite strategies from Hauser:

1. **Be nice to people, and they will trust you.** "Trust allows you to build relationships, and being successful in business is all about relationships," Hauser told me. "If you're an entrepreneur, relationships are critical. There are relationships with investors and clients. You might be building a team. And that all comes back to relational intelligence. If you are negotiating with an investor, or decision making, it all translates to trust.

   "My mother, an Italian immigrant, launched a very successful tailoring business, and she showed me how to lead with kindness and strength. She had that velvet glove. She could be very kind, but she could also be very direct when she needed to be. It is that balance of being kind, but at the same time not being wishy-washy. It's being very direct with what you want to get across without being a jerk. You don't want to burn bridges.

   "Every situation you're in as a business owner, approach it with the mindset that 'I am going to be kind, but I am also going to be strong. If I have to make a tough call, I am going to make it.'

"I had to make decisions all the time when we were launching People.com and some of them were not popular. One thing I would always do is get input from others, which showed them that 'I care about your opinion. I am going to listen to you.' But I had to stand in my own two shoes and make my own decision."

2. **Form a mentor circle.** "I have a lot of friends who are over 50, had a big job, and are now transitioning and launching startups. The thing that I hear the most is that 'I am just so lonely. I am in my house working on the concept of this business idea. I have people working for me remotely. We do phone calls every once in a while, but I miss not having support around me.' "I recommend trying to find other entrepreneurs – women and men – where you can get together.

"My friend Lesley Jane Seymour [the former editor of *More* magazine who launched CoveyClub.com for lifelong learners reinventing themselves] did this. She brings together 10 to 15 entrepreneurs. They rotate houses and get together once a month to work together. Some people work in the living room, some in the kitchen. They have speakers come in.

"I regularly host a mentor circle; it's around 15 women and we will meet for about an hour in a coffee shop or a coworking space. It's very informal. They end up getting to know each other and support each other."

3. **Create a formal advisory board and a personal board of directors.** "If you're starting a business, I recommend creating a formal advisory board of three or four people. You give some equity to the professionals you ask to join. It can be anywhere from ¼% up to 1%, and you have the person officially on board as an adviser. That way they have some skin in the game.

"Be very intentional about the kind of support that you need. If you're building a product that is heavily dependent on technology, but you are a marketer, you probably need to bring a tech-type person on as an adviser.

"Even before you start fundraising, have advisers; you don't even have to call it a board. Be very clear with these advisers about where you need their help. It could be opening doors. It could be helping you fundraise. It could be a functional area like technology. Having advisers gives you credibility when you are going out to fundraise.

"Your personal board of directors is a little bit different. For me, it is my husband, my best friend, and my executive coach. Those are the people who know me inside and out. They know what drives me. They know my values. They are my sounding board. They are the people I check in with when I am really unsure of what I should be doing."

4. **Make time for self-care.** "Self-care is something a lot of us struggle with, especially when you are starting a business – which is so all-consuming. For me, I know I do better when I set smaller goals for myself.

"It is so good for me, for example, when I meditate. I see the positive effect, but I don't have 20 minutes in the morning and 20 minutes at night to meditate. I do my five minutes. I have this great app, Meditation Studio, and I do it in the morning.

"I don't want to put pressure on myself and set unrealistic goals around self-care; then I end up feeling guilty and feel bad about myself. I would rather set goals like five minutes a day. With a more manageable goal, you are more likely to have a successful outcome."

Chapter Recap

In this chapter, we learned how a holistic veterinarian started a business manufacturing and selling horse muzzles with an eye to a viable retirement business. She saw a niche in her industry and went for it. You also learned about the importance of getting certified as a woman-owned business. Plus, you got a smattering of great advice from two entrepreneur experts besides me.

YOUR TO-DO LIST

- Do some sleuthing to see if there is a need for a product or service in the field you work in now.
- Consider getting certified as a woman-owned business.
- Start a mentor circle.
- Make time for yourself. Start a meditation practice. Walk your dog. Take regular "you" breaks.

Afterword

It takes a dream, a vision, a willingness to take risks. It requires a determination that can't be measured. But being your own boss, and working at and for the things you love and believe in, is what matters in life.

These efforts make us rich.

Sometimes this is work that does in fact make us financially rich. But importantly, there is the richness of the internal reward that, for all of the mid-life entrepreneurs I have featured in these pages, is far, far greater in the whole scheme of things.

Entrepreneurship means freedom. It means love. It means getting out of a comfort zone. It means creativity. It means destiny.

To me, all of these people's journeys to entrepreneurship are inspiring, energizing, and hopeful. Each person's motivation, challenges, and rewards are wildly different. Yet at the core of each one lies a heart.

My wish is that you have come to the end of this guide with a treasure chest of resources to help you successfully launch your own business. The path to entrepreneurship is a process that rarely results in an overnight sensation, but rather is a steady accumulation of rich moments. These rich moments – both personal and financial – make you smile and say, yes, I *am* doing just what I am supposed to be doing at this stage of my life.

This work matters. It is *rich.*

Index

Page numbers followed by *f* refer to figures.

Index

Index

Index

Index